FAMILY ADOPTION IN FLORIDA

A Self-Help Guide by Ruth Tick, FALDP, LLC

Grandparents, aunts, uncles, brothers, sisters may all adopt under Florida Statute Chapter 61.

NOTICE:

We have prepared this book to help pro se litigants complete the family law forms for a family adoption. We have used or made reference to the most current Florida Supreme Court approved forms when available. We have made every effort to make the instructions simple; and the comments helpful. Nothing we have written should be considered legal advice. And nothing we have written should be a substitute for legal advice or prevent anyone from seeking legal advice when necessary.

The information and the sample forms we have included are as up to date as possible -- and are current as of July 2016. Before relying on any of the forms or information, please check the Florida Supreme Court's website to make sure the forms included best apply to your situation. There may be additional or alternate forms that you need, depending on your local court rules, and your specific circumstances. The Florida Supreme Court's website is www.flcourts.org.

The authors, publishers, and/or The Florida Association of Legal Document Preparers, LLC (FALDP, LLC) will not be held responsible for errors, omissions, or mistakes that appear in this guide; and will be held harmless from any damage incurred by anyone using this book.

For information on bulk purchases, or affiliate sales please contact staff@faldp.org .

Dedication

This book is dedicated to all the good people caring for the children of others... to the step-parents, grandparents, siblings, aunts, and uncles who choose to do the right thing.
To the good people with
enough love in their hearts to embrace a relative's child as their own,
and give that child a solid place
in the world
and a better chance for a better life.

The Florida Association of Legal Document Preparers Mission Statement

We, the members of the Florida Association of Legal Document Preparers, deeply believe that it is the right of all American consumers to have access to the legal system, regardless of income or education. It is our mission to deliver well researched legal information to consumers.

The FALDP mission embodies our quest and our goals. We offer legal information; and document preparation assistance. We hope that by educating consumers about their legal rights -- we will have done our part to give others hope.

The FALDP mission is a journey. We have only begun, there is much to do. We hope that the confidence gained through education and knowledge will empower consumers, so they may have a fighting chance to enforce or pursue their rights in a court of law.

Table of Contents

FAMILY ADOPTION IN FLORIDA

A Self-Help Guide

Family Adoption ~ Stepparent, Grandparent, Aunts, Uncles, Brothers & Sisters; And What to Know About Gay Adoption

Introduction

In Florida, family adoptions are increasingly common. In many families, grandparents and other family members have taken care of their relative's children since birth. For a mix of reasons ranging from emotional to practical, individuals and couples seek to adopt a relative's child. Florida law allows family adoptions as long as the best interests of the child are upheld.

There are Florida Supreme Court approved forms to request the court to grant a stepparent adoption -- Joint Petition for Adoption by Stepparent is readily available online. A family adoption such as adoption by grandparents or adoption by a close blood relative is treated much the same way as a stepparent adoption. The main difference between a step-parent and any other family adoption (including a grandparent adoption) is that in a stepparent adoption only one of the natural parents must consent to the adoption. In a stepparent adoption one of the child's natural parents remains the legal parent, and the stepparent takes the place of the child's other natural parent.

In this guide we use the terms natural parents and biological parents interchangeably. Adoptive parents are the parents seeking to adopt the child. After the adoption is final, they are simply called parents. A family adoption is, just as it sounds, an adoption among family members. In Florida a family adoption is defined as an adoption between relatives within three degrees of relation by blood (consanguinity). In other words, a child's mother, brother, father, or sister is related by blood within one degree. A child's grandparents; and aunts and uncles who are siblings of the child's parents; are related by blood within two degrees.

The family adoptions discussed in this guide are governed by Florida Statute Chapter 63. The requirement for a background check, home study, and completion of the Model Approach to Partnerships in Parenting training (MAPP) are generally waived in family adoptions.

When all parties agree the process is manageable for people to do themselves. When you are representing yourself in a court action, you are proceeding pro se.

Family Adoption

Florida law provides a simple process for stepparent adoption, and forms for a stepparent adoption are readily available on the Florida Supreme Court's website, www.flcourts.org. However, there are no specific Florida Supreme Court approved forms for other family adoptions such as grandparent adoption. Other family adoptions such as grandparent adoptions fall under the same statutes as stepparent adoptions -- Florida Statute Chapter 63. Some of the forms included in this guide for stepparent adoption are identical to or nearly identical to the forms needed for other family adoptions. The relative adoption forms, which we located online, have proven to be acceptable in Florida circuits. Some circuits may require additional forms or different forms.

In a relative adoption it is common, although not required, that the relative or relatives have been the child's primary caregivers for a long time, sometimes since the child's birth. A common scenario is that the mother was young and unmarried when she gave birth, and finds that she is unable or ill-equipped to properly care for a baby. The natural father is often also young and unable to to accept parental responsibilities.

Usually at least one of the parents readily consents to a family adoption. The other parent may have distanced himself from the relationship and lost contact with the child. Often both natural parents agree that it is in the child's best interest to be adopted. Sometimes the other parent cannot be located in order to give consent; and sometimes the identity of the natural father is unknown. This guide provides information, suggestions, and procedures to navigate these situations.

The form central to the entire process is the Petition for Adoption. There are also forms that are must be filed with almost all adoptions, with some slight variations. The biological parent(s) consent is not always easy to obtain, sometimes the biological father's identity is unknown. And sometimes, the whereabouts of the biological mother or the biological father are not known. Either of these circumstances requires a diligent search to attempt to locate him or her before going forward. The adoptee's consent is required only when the child is at least twelve years old.

The forms associated with searching the putative father registry are always required - even when the child's parents were divorced and the father's identity is well known. This requirement seems illogical - and it is. However, understanding the purpose of the putative father registry will help you realize that it does serve a useful purpose. The putative father registry exists to protect the paternal rights of unwed fathers. The simplest way to understand its use, is to consider a circumstance where a couple broke up while the woman was pregnant, and the father lost track of the mother's whereabouts. If that father wants to be part of his child's life, he can register with the putative father registry to preserve his rights. Or, in a similar circumstance, if a couple breaks up while the mother is pregnant, but the father doesn't know, the child cannot be adopted without the search of the putative father registry and the father's consent.

There is generally one single hearing on a Petition for Adoption. The adoptive parent(s) are required to attend, but the parent(s) terminating parental rights are not required to appear. However, sometimes the parent(s) terminating parental rights chooses to attend.

Gay Adoption in Florida

There are no Florida Supreme Court approved forms for gay adoption in Florida, no cut and dry procedure. The procedures for stepparent adoption seem to be almost sufficient. It is common for one of the partners to be the biological parent or to have already adopted the child as a single parent. Adding the life partner as a second parent, similar to the procedures for a stepparent adoption seems to satisfy the court.

The law prohibiting gay people from adopting changed in June 2015. However, before the law officially changed in September 2010 a Third District Court of Appeals ruling created a sea change in how that law was enforced. The the Third DCA ruling affirmed a prior (2008) ruling in Miami-Dade which also found the law prohibiting gay citizens from adoption as unconstitutional.

Neither judge could reconcile the hypocrisy of the law to real life. At that time Florida was the only state to have a blanket statutory prohibition against gay adoption. Arkansas and Utah banned any unmarried (straight or gay) couples from adopting or fostering children. Mississippi banned gay couples, but not single gays, from adopting.

Commenting on the Third DCA ruling, Robert Rosenwald, lead counsel for the Florida American Civil Liberties Union (ACLU), stated:

"Clearly, Florida's law was the most draconian in the nation until today." The hypocrisy ran deep. At the same time that gays were prohibited from adopting; those same individuals were allowed to be foster parents. One argument in opposition to the adoption was that the children of gay parents would be stigmatized because of their parents' homosexuality. If that argument followed logic, then wouldn't the foster children of gays be similarly stigmatized? Either both statements must be true; or neither statement is true.

Judge Cindy S. Lederman of Miami ruled in 2008 that the ban on gay adoption violated the adoptive father's rights under the of the U.S. Constitution. The 14th Amendment, Section I states:

> *"No state shall make or enforce any law which shall abridge the privileges or immunities of citizens of the United States; nor shall any state deprive any person of life, liberty, or property, without due process of law; nor deny to any person within its jurisdiction the equal protection of the laws."*

In all Florida adoptions, except for family adoptions, the adoptive parents must be approved by the Department of Children and Families (DCF). Adoptive parents must pass a background check and undergo a home study. Prohibiting an adoption based solely on whether an adoptive parent is gay; is like prohibiting an adoption based on an adoptive parent's race.

In Judge Gerald B. Cope Jr.'s 35 page Third DCA opinion, he stated: "It is difficult to see any rational basis in utilizing homosexual persons as foster parents or guardians on a temporary or permanent basis, while imposing a blanket prohibition on adoption by those same persons." (In re Adoption of X.X.G.)

Soon after Judge Cope's ruling Governor Charlie Crist announced that the state of Florida will immediately cease enforcing the ban on gay adoption. In June 2015 Florida officially amended the Florida Statutes to allow gay people to adopt.

Currently, Florida does not allow a biological mother to put her wife's name on the child's birth certificate. That means the biological mother's wife has no parental rights when their child is born even when she is married to the biological mother. Note: this is different than opposite-sex married couples. A man married to a woman is presumed to be the biological father when the woman gives birth.

Married lesbian couples can do a stepparent adoption after the child's birth to ensure that the biological parent's wife has full equal parental rights to the child. Perhaps this will change in the future so that same-sex couples are treated more like opposite-sex couples, but in the meantime, getting an adoption best protects the non-biological parent's rights. Similarly, married gay men, where one is the biological father, can do a stepparent adoption so that the minor child is the legal child of both.

Without a stepparent adoption, the non-biological parent in a same-sex family might have no legal rights to the child. None. Marriage alone does not guarantee equal rights to the child when one spouse is the biological parent and the other is not. It's also not enough for the non-biological parent to be set up as the guardian of the child.

The only sure way for the non-biological parent to obtain legal rights to the child in Florida is through a stepparent adoption or to jointly adopt together at the same time.

A stepparent adoption lets the non-biological parent make important decisions and share in custody for the child even if the couple separates or if one parent dies. Or it could be much simpler: it will let the non-biological parent do things like pick up their child from school or make medical decisions when the biological parent can't be reached.

Adoption Scenarios

The following are just a few possible adoption scenarios. There are many more. These examples may help illustrate some of the possible circumstances which lead to a family adoption.

Stepparent Adoption - Jack and Jill got married three months after graduation from high school, and divorced their second year of college. In those few years, they quickly found that their marriage and maturity levels were not up to raising a family. Although they both loved their baby dearly, it was just too hard to go on with work, school, and raising baby Kevin. They agreed to divorce and Jill and baby Kevin moved back in with Jill's Mom and Dad. For the next few years, Jack was as attentive as he could be, and helped out with Kevin's expenses as well as he could. After a while, the pair drifted farther apart. Jill met Allen three years after she and Jack went their separate ways. After a six month courtship they married. When Jill called Jack to announce the news, she also asked him if he would agree to a stepparent adoption. He did. Jill sent him the consent form as an email attachment, which Jack promptly signed, notarized, and returned. Jack was secretly relieved, as he had realized early on that he wasn't being a good father. He meant to, but didn't really know how. Jack felt a sickening feeling of guilt sometimes, because he knew he wasn't making enough money to support a child. At 24, Jack had made the first truly adult decision of his life. It hurt his heart to know that another man would be his son's father. Jack had met Allen a couple of times, and he seemed like a straight up guy. Jill was certainly in love with him. Jack realized that given the circumstances, the best thing that he could do for his son, was to let him go.

Grandparent Adoption - Kelly thought she could be a single Mom. She had ignored her parents when they had told her not to get involved with a man that she wasn't going to marry. She had also ignored her parents advice when she didn't leave her boyfriend even though she knew he was cheating. In fact, she got angry at her parents when they told her to leave him, and then didn't speak to her parents for some months. But, when she found herself pregnant, and the man she thought loved her left town with someone else. -- heartbroken and pregnant -- she went back home to her parents house. They took her in and took care of her. Her first intention was to have the baby and raise it herself. Her parents suggested that she give the baby up for adoption, and Kelly even went so far as to call an agency. She made the call to please her parents, but her heart wasn't in it. She wanted to keep her baby, someone to love her for her for always.

Kelly's parents made it clear, that she could move back home, but it was Kelly's responsibility to take care of the baby and provide for her. The first few months of being a new mom were fun and exciting, everything the baby did was sweet and enchanting. Kelly didn't mind it one bit when the baby cried in the middle of the night, she got up, rocked her back to sleep and went back to bed. When the baby turned three months old, her mother sat down with Kelly at the kitchen table and told Kelly that maternity leave was over. It was time for Kelly to get a job.

Kelly found a job quickly, and for the first two months Kelly's Mom watched the baby for free. Then Kelly's Mom informed her that she would no longer be able to watch the baby and that Kelly needed to find a daycare. And she did. There was a daycare close to Kelly's workplace that had flexible hours, which helped a lot, since Kelly was working as a server. Sometimes Kelly had to work breakfast and lunch shift, and other times the dinner shift. It wasn't long before Kelly realized that most of the money she earned was going for daycare and taking care of the baby in general. She didn't resent it, it was just hard. She asked her parents for more help, and they said no, we're already giving you all the help we can.

Finally, Kelly screwed up her courage and asked her parents if they would consider adopting her baby. They said yes, and that they had been hoping that she would ask. To Kelly their consent was a miracle. Now she would still be able to know her baby (as a sister), and know that her baby was being taken care of by two people that already loved her.

Aunt and Uncle Adoption - Natalie was distraught and in mourning when she gave birth. Her husband, George, had died a sudden and violent death while she was in her seventh month of pregnancy. When the baby was just two months old she flew from Michigan to Florida to visit her sister, Cheryl, for Thanksgiving. The day after Thanksgiving Natalie asked her sister if she could keep the baby for a few months while she got over the shock of George's death. Cheryl and her husband, Mark, readily agreed to keep the baby temporarily. They quickly fell in love with their niece, Rosa, who was an outgoing lively baby. And, although Cheryl and Mark had not intended to fall so helplessly in love, there it was. Back in Michigan, Natalie, rather than recovering from her husband's death, fell deeper into a black depression and struggled to get out of bed every morning. Natalie felt she couldn't continue life without George and thought she might just end it. When she told her therapist that she felt that life was not worth living, he promptly ordered her into a mental health facility. As soon as Natalie called Cheryl with the news that she was in a mental health facility and being treated for suicidal depression, Cheryl asked if she could adopt Rosa. Natalie agreed that it was a good idea for the adults, and there was no question that it was the best possible decision for Rosa.

Gay Adoption - Gina and Lori met when Lori's daughter, Alice, was three years old. Lori and the biological father, Dennis, had never been married, and had split up during Lori's pregnancy. Dennis very likely didn't even know he was a father. Lori had come out as a lesbian at the time of their break up and was quite happy that he didn't know he was a father. Lori had never contacted Dennis or asked him for anything. And, by the time she met Gina, Lori had completely lost track of Dennis. Gina and Lori moved in together and shared the household responsibility and raised Alice together as a family. They married as soon as same sex marriage became legal in Florida. Several months after gay marriage became legal, the law prohibiting gay people from adopting was also changed. They consulted with several attorneys, who wanted retainers ranging from $2500. on up to $10,000. And, although these attorneys came highly recommended by others in the gay community, they didn't seem to be particularly knowledgeable about gay adoption specifically, or even adoptions in general.

Gina, who was a graduate student studying criminal justice, took to the internet to find out more about adoption. She discovered that the process for stepparent adoption should work just fine, but that there were not Florida Supreme Court approved forms for a same sex stepparent adoption. But, she was able to adapt the forms by changing all of the gender specific terms to conform to their situation.

Next since they did not have a current address for Dennis, they went through the steps for a diligent search, and prepared the Affidavit of Diligent Search along with the other required forms. They were not able to locate Dennis in a search, so they then prepared a Notice of Action. The Notice of Action allowed them to publish a legal notice of their intention for stepparent adoption. They published the legal notice for four consecutive weeks in their local paper. Dennis never came forward. They then filed a Motion and Order for Default with the clerk of court. The motion for default states to the court that although Dennis was properly served (by constructive service) he failed to respond to the court in any way. The adoption went forward, and granted by the judge.

Stepparent Adoption, Default - Another possible scenario is when the biological father was properly served with the petition for stepparent adoption and associated documents and failed to answer. Myra and John had two daughters together, but never married. After their break up, John moved away and Myra lost track of him. When she married Adam they decided that Adam should adopt Myra's girls who were now four and five years old. Adam was the only father they knew. And Myra wanted to make sure that should anything happen to her, the girls would be properly taken care of - by Adam. After a diligent search, Myra located John in prison. It is always possible to serve someone in prison, although each facility may have their own rules about the exact procedure. The process server served John in prison and filed the Return of Service with the clerk of court. Myra then prepared and filed a Motion and Order for Default. At the hearing, the adoption was granted.

Frequently Asked Questions

Are there any forms besides the forms in this book that I need?

Maybe. Some circuits have special requirements that do not apply elsewhere. Check with the clerk of court to see if there is a checklist for family adoptions. We did not include the Application for Search of the Putative Father Registry which is a Department of Health form. Some circuits require that you file it with your initial filing. That form is available here - http://www.floridahealth.gov/certificates/certificates/birth/Putative_Father/index.html

How much is the filing fee?

At the time of this writing, the filing fee is $442. Check with your local clerk of court ahead of time to be sure that nothing has changed.

Can I apply for indigent status and request to have my filing fees waived?

Yes, you can apply for indigent status for a family adoption just as you would for any civil court filing. The clerk of court has the form, or you can download it from http://www.faldp.org/civil-indigent.html

What if I have lost contact with my adoptive child's parent? How do I notify him or her of the adoption?

If you do not know where a parent is, you will have to conduct a Diligent Search. If you are unable to find the parent you then file an Affidavit of Diligent Search. You will then be allowed to publish your legal intent to adopt. This is called constructive service. The legal notice must be published for four consecutive weeks in a periodical with at least 20,000 in circulation.

In a gay adoption what will go on the child's birth certificate?

After the stepparent adoption is complete, both of the names of the same-sex couple.. That means both moms or both dads. Once the stepparent adoption is complete, or if the couple adopts jointly at the same time, a new birth certificate is issued by Florida showing the names of the new legal parents. The names will be listed as "Parent 1" and "Parent 2."

What is a certified copy of a court order?

A certified copy from the clerk of court bears a clerk's certification stamp. A copy of any court document costs $1.00 per page; and the certification costs an additional $2.00 for each document. A document may have multiple pages, but only needs one certification.

CHECKLIST FOR STEPPARENT AND OTHER FAMILY ADOPTIONS

This checklist is here to help you with the procedure for bringing your case to court.

A. Required fees:

- The Clerk of Court can give you information on filing fees. If you are unable to pay those fees you may ask the clerk for an Affidavit of Indigency. If you qualify for indigent status your filing fees may be waived.
- Filing fee paid, or fee waiver granted by the Clerk of Court.

B. Cover Sheet:

- Family Law Civil Cover Sheet - Choose "Adoption under Chapter 63" from the list.

C. Petition.

- Joint Petition for Adoption by Stepparent.
- OR: Joint Petition for Adoption by Relative(s) or Petition for Adoption by Relative (Individual)

Note: A certified copy of the minor's original birth certificate must be filed with the petition.

D. **Required** forms to be filed with the petition:

- Uniform Child Custody Jurisdiction and Enforcement Act Affidavit (UCCJEA) - This is a federal form required in most family law cases which involve children. It documents where the child has resided for the past five years; and makes sure that there are no conflicting court orders from any other state or jurisdiction.

- Indian Child Welfare Act Affidavit-Form - This is a 1978 federal form that discloses whether the child is being adopted from an Indian reservation or is a member of any Indian tribe.

- Motion for Search of Putative Father Registry - This form and process is required in all Florida family adoptions, even when the identity of the father is known.

- Order for Search of Putative Father Registry - This is the accompanying order for the motion to search the putative father registry. It is submitted as a proposed order for the judge to sign.

- Application for Search of the Putative Father Registry - This is a Department of Health and Vital Statistics form that is sent directly to that agency after the judge signs the Order to Search the Putative Father Registry. This form has been omitted from this book, however you can download it from the site for the Department of Health and Vital Statistics -
http://www.floridahealth.gov/certificates/certificates/birth/Putative_Father/index.html
Form DH1963

- Consent from Parent(s) and Termination of Parental Rights - Most family adoptions are consensual and it isn't difficult to obtain a consent from the biological parent(s). The same form also terminates the parent's rights. It must be witnessed by two people and be notarized. Occasionally someone will obtain the form well in advance of filing a petition for adoption. Some circuits have ruled that the signed consent form is valid for up to one year prior to filing the petition for adoption.

- Consent from Adoptee - Children age twelve and up must consent to the adoption. In addition to consenting to the adoption, children age twelve and up also must consent to their name change. The consent to name change is done on the same form.

D. Forms that may be required:

- Summons for Service of Process on an Individual; and Process Server Memorandum - If you have a valid address for a biological parent and he or she has not returned a signed Consent from Parent that you provided, you will need to have the biological parent served by a sheriff or private process server.

- Motion and Order for Default - If you have the biological parent served and the parent does not respond in any way to you and to the Court, you the prepare and file the Motion and Order for Default. This says to the court that the person was served, but failed to provide an answer or response. That way your case can continue without that parent's participation.

- Affidavit of Diligent Search - If you do not have a current address for the biological parent, you need to conduct a search. Different counties have different local rules as to how many places you must search. Some counties require that you search in all of the places listed on the affidavit, others require a search of only a few. The point is that you need to conduct a **diligent search** to show the clerk of court that you really tried to locate the biological parent. If you happen to find the biological parent through your search efforts, you will either contact him or her to request a signature on the Consent form; or have the parent served by a process server. If you are not able to find the parent during the diligent search, you then request from the clerks the authority to serve by constructive service. This is done by filing a Notice of Action form. You can have a private investigator conduct the search for you, but you are not required to do so.

- Notice of Action - If after conducting a Diligent Search and Inquiry and failing to locate the biological parent, you may then file the Notice of Action. The Notice of Action allows you to publish your legal intent to adopt. The legal notice must be published for four consecutive weeks in a periodical with at least 20,000 circulation. The periodical does not have to be a daily newspaper, it can be a weekly shopper type paper that accepts legal notices. After the four consecutive weeks of publication and the biological parent not coming forward, you then file the Motion and Order for Default as explained above.

STEP BY STEP

1	First gather all information you'll need, such as all parties addresses and full names. Also make sure you have a certified copy of the child's birth certificate. You'll have to provide it to the court at the time of filing.
2	Next, complete all paperwork in the Required Forms section of this book. If your intention is a family adoption, other than a stepparent adoption, use either the Joint Petition for Adoption by Relatives; or Petition for Adoption by Relative, instead of the petition form designed for a stepparent adoption.
3	Third, sign the forms in front of a notary. All forms that have a notary area (called a "jurat") need to be notarized. Then make at least one set of copies of all documents.
4	File all forms with the clerk of court in the county where the child resides. At the time of filing, you will also pay the filing fee which is currently $442.00. Wait a few days and contact the clerk of court to see what you need to do to set up a court hearing. The process to set a hearing varies by county and circuit. After the judge signs the Order for Search of the Putative Father Registry, you may be required to forward that order to the Department of Health and Vital Statistics. Or, in some circuits, the clerk will do it for you. There is a small additional fee payable to the Department of Health for the search. Prior to the hearing the biological parent or parents have either signed a consent form, been served, or been searched for unsuccessfully and have been notified of the pending adoption by publication.
5	There is generally one single hearing for a family adoption. The adoptive parents are required to appear, but the child or children are not. Sometimes the biological parents choose to appear, even though they already signed a consent to the adoption, but they are not required to do so. At the hearing, the judge may sign the order granting the adoption, or the judge may send it in the mail after the hearing.
6	The clerks of court routinely seal the court record ten days after the judge sings the adoption order. During that ten day window the adoptive parents need to go to the courthouse and request several certified copies of the adoption order. The number of copies to request depends on the age of the child and how many activities the child is involved in. Each entity that affects that child's life will need a certified copy of the order of adoption. And each entity will need to keep that certified copy of the order of adoption for their records. The Department of Health and Vital Statistics, the Social Security Administration, the child's school, the child's doctor, and any other entities that the child is involved with, even sports clubs, will need a certified copy of the order of adoption. It is far better to request too many certified copies than not enough. If for any reason, a parent needs another copy of the order of adoption and the record has been sealed, a court order is required to unseal the record and obtain another certified copy of the order of adoption.

How to make pdf forms “fillable”

We know how difficult and confusing filling out legal forms can be. We also know your frustration is complete when you try to fill out Florida family law PDF forms and discover that the forms are not fillable. (We know fillable is not a real word – we mean interactive). These instructions teach you how to enter information into the PDF forms regardless of whether those little boxes exist. So when you see a PDF form that is not fillable, go through these steps.

First, download an alternate PDF program called **Foxit.** Here is the download link http://www.foxitsoftware.com/downloads/index.php. All you need is the free Foxit Reader. Look through the list and find the correct download for your operating system. Then install it to your computer.

Second, open the unfillable form using foxit. If you also have Adobe Acrobat Reader installed you may need to right click and choose “open with” Foxit in order to open your document with Foxit.

Third, look at the top right, just under the Foxit Tool Bar, and click on "Enable Editing". (Some forms are locked and will not allow editing at all.)

Fourth, click on the "T" for typewriter. in the center of the Foxit toolbar then place your cursor where you want to type. Once you click to begin, the toolbar changes and you will be able to change the font, size, etc.

Note, you will need to save the unfillable form to your computer before you'll be able to reopen and type into it. You still will not be able to remove anything that is already on the form, but you can easily type into the blanks.

The two fonts that are used in Florida court filings are 12 point Times New Roman; or 11 point Calibri.

If this has helped you, please let us know! 800-515-0496 ~ staff@faldp.org

APPENDIX I - REQUIRED FORMS

The forms on the next several pages are required in all or most family adoptions. It may not seem logical that the Motion for Search of the Putative Father Registry and the accompanying order should be required when the biological father's identity is know. However, the rules say that this search and these forms are required in all Florida adoptions. We have omitted the Application for Search of the Putative Father Registry which may also be required. That form can be downloaded from the Department of Health and Vital Statistics site - here:

http://www.floridahealth.gov/certificates/certificates/birth/Putative_Father/index.html

Sometimes an adoptive parent may initially believe that the biological parent will cooperate, only to discover that he or she won't return the Consent from Parent form. If that happens the biological parent will need to be served. The documents to have someone served are included in the second set of forms - "Supplemental Forms".

INSTRUCTIONS FOR FLORIDA FAMILY LAW RULES OF PROCEDURE FORM 12.928, COVER SHEET FOR FAMILY COURT CASES (11/13)

When should this form be used?

The Cover Sheet for Family Court Cases and the information contained in it neither replace nor supplement the filing and service of pleadings or other documents as required by law. This form shall be filed by the petitioner/party opening or reopening a case for the use of the **clerk of the circuit court** for the purpose of reporting judicial workload data pursuant to Florida Statutes section 25.075.

This form should be typed or printed in black ink. The petitioner must **file** this cover sheet with the first pleading or motion filed to open or reopen a case in all domestic and juvenile cases.

What should I do next?

Follow these instructions for completing the form:

I. Case Style. Enter the name of the court, the appropriate case number assigned at the time of filing of the original petition, the name of the judge assigned (if applicable), and the name (last, first, middle initial) of the petitioner(s) and respondent(s).

II. Type of Action /Proceeding. Place a check beside the proceeding you are initiating. If you are simultaneously filing more than one type of proceeding against the same opposing party, such as a modification and an enforcement proceeding, complete a separate cover sheet for each action being filed.

A) Initial Action/Petition
B) Reopening Case. If you check "Reopening Case," indicate whether you are filing a modification or supplemental petition or an action for enforcement by placing a check beside the appropriate action/petition.
    1. Modification/Supplemental Petition
    2. Motion for Civil Contempt/ Enforcement
    3. Other – All reopening actions not involving modification/supplemental petitions or petition enforcement.

III. Type of Case. Place a check beside the appropriate case. If the case fits more than one category, select the most definitive. Definitions of the categories are provided below.
A) Simplified Dissolution of Marriage- petitions for the termination of marriage pursuant to Florida Family Law Rule of Procedure 12.105.
B) Dissolution of Marriage - petitions for the termination of marriage pursuant to Chapter 61, Florida Statutes, other than simplified dissolution.
C) Domestic Violence - all matters relating to injunctions for protection against domestic violence pursuant to section 741.30, Florida Statutes.
D) Dating Violence - all matters relating to injunctions for protection against dating violence pursuant to section 784.046, Florida Statutes.

E) Repeat Violence - all matters relating to injunctions for protection against repeat violence pursuant to section 784.046, Florida Statutes.

F) Sexual Violence - all matters relating to injunctions for protection against sexual violence pursuant to section 784.046, Florida Statutes.

G) Stalking-all matters relating to injunctions for protection against stalking pursuant to section 784.0485, Florida Statutes

H) Support - IV-D - all matters relating to child or spousal support in which an application for assistance has been filed with the Department of Revenue, Child Support Enforcement under Title IV-D, Social Security Act, except for such matters relating to dissolution of marriage petitions (sections 409.2564, 409.2571, and 409.2597, Florida Statutes), paternity, or UIFSA.

I) Support-Non IV-D - all matters relating to child or spousal support in which an application for assistance has **not** been filed under Title IV-D, Social Security Act.

J) UIFSA- IV-D - all matters relating to Chapter 88, Florida Statutes, in which an application for assistance has been filed under Title IV-D, Social Security Act.

K) UIFSA - Non IV-D - all matters relating to Chapter 88, Florida Statutes, in which an application for assistance has **not** been filed under Title IV-D, Social Security Act.

L) Other Family Court - all matters involving time-sharing and/or parenting plans relating to minor child(ren), support unconnected with dissolution of marriage, annulment, delayed birth certificates pursuant to Florida Statutes section 382.0195, expedited affirmation of parental status pursuant to Florida Statutes section 742.16, termination of parental rights proceedings pursuant to Florida Statutes section 63.087, declaratory judgment actions related to premarital, marital, post-marital agreements, or other matters not included in the categories above.

M) Adoption Arising Out Of Chapter 63 - all matters relating to adoption pursuant to Chapter 63, Florida Statutes, excluding any matters arising out of Chapter 39, Florida Statutes.

N) Name Change - all matters relating to name change, pursuant to section 68.07, Florida Statutes.

O) Paternity/Disestablishment of Paternity – all matters relating to paternity pursuant to Chapter 742, Florida Statutes.

P) Juvenile Delinquency - all matters relating to juvenile delinquency pursuant to Chapter 985, Florida Statutes.

Q) Petition for Dependency - all matters relating to petitions for dependency.

R) Shelter Petition – all matters relating to shelter petitions pursuant to Chapter 39, Florida Statutes.

S) Termination of Parental Rights Arising Out Of Chapter 39 – all matters relating to termination of parental rights pursuant to Chapter 39, Florida Statutes.

T) Adoption Arising Out Of Chapter 39 – all matters relating to adoption pursuant to Chapter 39, Florida Statutes.

U) CINS/FINS – all matters relating to children in need of services (and families in need of services) pursuant to Chapter 984, Florida Statutes.

ATTORNEY OR PARTY SIGNATURE. Sign the Cover Sheet for Family Court Cases. Print legibly the name of the person signing the Cover Sheet for Family Court Cases. Attorneys must include a Florida Bar number. Insert the date the Cover Sheet for Family Court Cases is signed. Signature is a certification that filer has provided accurate information on the Cover Sheet for Family Court Cases.

Nonlawyer Remember, a person who is NOT an attorney is called a nonlawyer. If a nonlawyer helps you fill out these forms, that person must give you a copy of **Disclosure from Nonlawyer**, Florida Family Law Rules of Procedure Form 12.900(a), before he or she helps you. A nonlawyer helping you fill out these forms also **must**

put his or her name, address, and telephone number on the bottom of the last page of every form he or she helps you complete.

Where can I look for more information?

Before proceeding, you should read "General Information for Self-Represented Litigants" found at the beginning of these forms. For further information, see Rule 12.100, Florida Family Law Rules of Procedure.

COVER SHEET FOR FAMILY COURT CASES

I. Case Style

IN THE CIRCUIT COURT OF THE ______ JUDICIAL CIRCUIT,
IN AND FOR __________________ COUNTY, FLORIDA

Case No.: ________________
Judge: __________________

____
Petitioner

and

____
Respondent

II. Type of Action/Proceeding. Place a check beside the proceeding you are initiating. If you are simultaneously filing more than one type of proceeding against the same opposing party, such as a modification and an enforcement proceeding, complete a separate cover sheet for each action being filed. **If you are reopening a case, choose one of the three options below it.**

A) ____ Initial Action/Petition
B) ____ Reopening Case
   1. ____ Modification/Supplemental Petition
   2. ____ Motion for Civil Contempt/Enforcement
   3. ____ Other

III. Type of Case. If the case fits more than one type of case, select the most definitive.

A) ____ Simplified Dissolution of Marriage
B) ____ Dissolution of Marriage
C) ____ Domestic Violence
D) ____ Dating Violence
E) ____ Repeat Violence
F) ____ Sexual Violence
G) ____ Stalking
H) ____ Support IV-D (Department of Revenue, Child Support Enforcement)
I) ____ Support Non-IV-D (**not** Department of Revenue, Child Support Enforcement)
J) ____ UIFSA IV-D (Department of Revenue, Child Support Enforcement)
K) ____ UIFSA Non-IV-D (**not** Department of Revenue, Child Support Enforcement)
L) ____ Other Family Court
M) ____ Adoption Arising Out Of Chapter 63
N) ____ Name Change
O) ____ Paternity/Disestablishment of Paternity
P) ____ Juvenile Delinquency

Q) ____ Petition for Dependency
R) ____ Shelter Petition
S) ____ Termination of Parental Rights Arising Out Of Chapter 39
T) ____ Adoption Arising Out Of Chapter 39
U) ____ CINS/FINS

IV. Rule of Judicial Administration 2.545(d) requires that a Notice of Related Cases Form, Family Law Form 12.900(h), be filed with the initial pleading/petition by the filing attorney or self-represented litigant in order to notify the court of related cases. Is Form 12.900(h) being filed with this Cover Sheet for Family Court Cases and initial pleading/petition?

____ No, to the best of my knowledge, no related cases exist.
____ Yes, all related cases are listed on Family Law Form 12.900(h).

ATTORNEY OR PARTY SIGNATURE

I CERTIFY that the information I have provided in this cover sheet is accurate to the best of my knowledge and belief.

Signature______________________________ FL Bar No.: ____________________
Attorney or party (Bar number,if attorney)

______________________________ ____________________
(Type or print name) (E-mail Address(es))

____
Date

IF A NONLAWYER HELPED YOU FILL OUT THIS FORM, HE/SHE MUST FILL IN THE BLANKS BELOW: [fill in **all** blanks]
This form was prepared for the: *{choose only **one**}* ( ) Petitioner ( ) Respondent
This form was completed with the assistance of:
*{name of individual}*____,
{name of business} ____,
*{address}*____,
*{city}*________________, *{state}*______, *{telephone number }*________________.

INSTRUCTIONS FOR FLORIDA SUPREME COURT APPROVED FAMILY LAW FORM 12.981(b)(1), JOINT PETITION FOR ADOPTION BY STEPPARENT (11/15)

When should this form be used?

This form should be used when a stepparent is adopting his or her **spouse**'s child. Both the stepparent and his or her spouse must sign this **petition**. You must attach all necessary consents or acknowledgments that apply to your case, as listed under the Special Notes section below. Florida Statutes require that consent to adoption be obtained from:

B) The mother of the minor.

C) The father of the minor if:

II. The minor was conceived or born while the father was married to the mother;
III. The minor is his child by adoption;
IV. The minor has been established by a court proceeding to be his child;
V. He has filed an affidavit of paternity pursuant to section 382.013(2)(c) Florida Statutes; or
VI. In the case of an unmarried biological father, he has acknowledged in writing, signed in the presence of a competent witness, that he is the father of the minor, has filed such acknowledgment with the Office of Vital Statistics of the Department of Health within the required timeframes, and has complied with the requirements of section 63.062(2), Florida Statutes.

Determining whether someone's consent is required, or when consent may not be required is a complicated issue and you may wish to consult an attorney. For more information about consenting to adoption, you should refer to Chapter 63, Florida Statutes, and sections 63.062-63.082 in particular.

This form should be typed or printed in black ink. The name to be given to the child(ren) **after** the adoption should be used in the heading of the petition. The stepparent is the **petitioner**, because he or she is the one who is asking the court for legal action. After completing this form, you and your spouse must sign it before a **notary public** or **deputy clerk**. You should then **file** the original and 1 copy with the **clerk of the circuit court** in the county where the minor resides unless the court changes the venue.

IMPORTANT INFORMATION REGARDING E-FILING

The Florida Rules of Judicial Administration now require that all petitions, pleadings, and documents be filed electronically except in certain circumstances. **Self-represented litigants may file petitions or other pleadings or documents electronically; however, they are not required to do so.** If you choose to file your pleadings or documents electronically, you must do so in accordance with Florida Rule of Judicial Administration 2.525, and you must follow the procedures of the judicial circuit in which you file. **The rules and procedures should be carefully read and followed.**

What should I do next?

For your case to proceed, you must have the written consent of the other birth parent and the child, if applicable. The **court** may choose not to require consent to an adoption in some circumstances. For more information about situations where consent may not be required, see section 63.064, Florida Statutes. If you are attempting to proceed without the consent of the other birth parent, you may wish to consult with an attorney. Section 63.054, Florida Statutes, requires that in each adoption proceeding, the Florida Putative Father Registry be searched. You will need an order from the judge to do this, which you can request by filing a **Motion for Search of the Putative Father Registry,** Florida Supreme Court Approved Family Law Form 12.981(a)(6)**.**

When you have filed all of the required forms and met the requirements as outlined above, you are ready to set a **hearing** on your petition. You should check with the clerk of court, **family law intake staff** or the **judicial assistant** to set a **final hearing**. If all persons required to consent have consented and the consents/affidavits of nonpaternity have been filed with the court, the hearing may be held immediately. If not, notice of the hearing must be given as provided by the Rules of Civil Procedure. See Form 1.902, Florida Rules of Civil Procedure. If you know where the other birth parent lives, you should use **personal service.** If you absolutely do not know where he or she lives, you may use **constructive service**. In order to use constructive service you will need to complete and submit to the court **Stepparent Adoption: Affidavit of Diligent Search**, Florida Supreme Court Approved Family Law Form 12.981(a)(4). For more information about personal and constructive service, you should refer to the **"General Instructions for Self-Represented Litigants"** found at the beginning of these forms and the instructions to Florida Family Law Rules of Procedure Forms 12.910(a) and 12.913(b) and Florida Supreme Court Approved Family Law Form 12.913(a). However, the law regarding constructive service is very complex and you may wish to consult an attorney regarding that issue.

Where can I look for more information?

Before proceeding, you should read "General Information for Self-Represented Litigants" found at the beginning of these forms. See Chapter 63, Florida Statutes, and Florida Family Law Rule 12.200(a)(2) for further information.

IMPORTANT INFORMATION REGARDING E-SERVICE ELECTION

After the initial service of process of the petition or supplemental petition by the Sheriff or certified process server, the Florida Rules of Judicial Administration now require that all documents required or permitted to be served on the other party must be served by electronic mail (e-mail) except in certain circumstances. **You must strictly comply with the format requirements set forth in the Rules of Judicial Administration.** If you elect to participate in electronic service, which means serving or receiving pleadings by electronic mail (e-mail), or through the Florida Courts E-Filing Portal, you **must** review Florida Rule of Judicial Administration 2.516. You may find this rule at www.flcourts.org through the link to the Rules of Judicial Administration provided under either Family Law Forms: Getting Started, or Rules of Court in the A-Z Topical Index.

SELF-REPRESENTED LITIGANTS MAY SERVE DOCUMENTS BY E-MAIL; HOWEVER, THEY ARE NOT REQUIRED TO DO SO. If a self-represented litigant elects to serve and receive documents by e-mail, the procedures must always be followed once the initial election is made.

To serve and receive documents by e-mail, you must designate your e-mail addresses by using the **Designation of Current Mailing and E-mail Address**, Florida Supreme Court Approved Family Law Form 12.915, and you must provide your e-mail address on each form on which your signature appears. Please **CAREFULLY** read the rules and instructions for: **Certificate of Service (General),** Florida Supreme Court Approved Family Law Form 12.914; **Designation of Current Mailing and E-mail Address**, Florida Supreme Court Approved Family Law Form 12.915; and Florida Rule of Judicial Administration 2.516.

Special notes...

With this petition you must file the following:

1. Consent form executed by the birth parent, **Stepparent Adoption**: **Consent and Waiver by Parent,** Florida Supreme Court Approved Family Law Form 12.981(a)(1) or **Stepparent Adoption**: **Affidavit of Nonpaternity,** Florida Supreme Court Approved Family Law Form 12.981(a)(3).
2. If any person whose consent is required is deceased, a certified copy of the death certificate must be attached to this Petition.
3. Consent form executed by the minor child(ren), if the child(ren) is/are over 12 years of age, **Stepparent Adoption: Consent of Adoptee,** Florida Supreme Court Approved Family Law Form 12.981(a)(2)**.** The court can excuse filing of this form under certain circumstances.
4. Certified copy of the child(ren)'s birth certificate.
5. **Uniform Child Custody Jurisdiction and Enforcement Act (UCCJEA) Affidavit**, Florida Supreme Court Approved Family Law Form 12.902(d).
6. If applicable, **Stepparent Adoption: Motion for Search of the Putative Father Registry,** Florida Supreme Court Approved Family Law Form 12.981(a)(6).

These family law forms contain a **Final Judgment of Stepparent Adoption**, Florida Supreme Court Approved Family Law Form 12.981(b)(2), which the judge may use. You should check with the clerk, family law intake staff, or judicial assistant to see if you need to bring a final judgment form with you to the hearing. If so, you should type or print the heading, including the circuit, county case number, division, and the child(ren)'s names, and leave the rest blank for the judge to complete at your hearing. You should decide how many **certified copies** of the final judgment you will need and be prepared to obtain them after the hearing. There is a charge for certified copies, and the clerk can tell you how much. The file will be sealed after the final hearing, and then it will take an order from a judge to open the file and obtain a copy of the final judgment.

AN ADOPTIVE STEPPARENT WILL CONTINUE TO HAVE PARENTAL RIGHTS, INCLUDING CUSTODY AND TIME-SHARING, WHERE APPROPRIATE, IN THE EVENT OF A LATER DISSOLUTION OF MARRIAGE, AND MAY BE LIABLE FOR CHILD SUPPORT IN THE EVENT OF A LATER DISSOLUTION OF MARRIAGE. YOU COULD BE

LIABLE IN LITIGATION FOR THE ACTIONS OF THE ADOPTEE(S). THIS ADOPTION MAY ALSO AFFECT THE ADOPTEE'S INHERITANCE.

Remember, a person who is NOT an attorney is called a nonlawyer. If a nonlawyer helps you fill out these forms, that person must give you a copy of a **Disclosure from Nonlawyer**, Florida Family Law Rules of Procedure Form 12.900 (a), before he or she helps you. A nonlawyer helping you fill out these forms also **must** put his or her name, address, and telephone number on the bottom of the last page of every form he or she helps you complete.

IN THE CIRCUIT COURT OF THE ________________ JUDICIAL CIRCUIT,
IN AND FOR ________________ COUNTY, FLORIDA

Case No.:
____
Division:
____

IN THE MATTER OF THE ADOPTION OF

____,
{use name to be given to the minor child} Adoptee.

JOINT PETITION FOR ADOPTION BY STEPPARENT

Petitioner, *{full legal name}* ____________________________________, being sworn, joined by the above-named child(ren)'s _____ mother _____ father, *{full legal name}* _________________________, being sworn, files this joint petition for adoption of the above-named minor child(ren), under chapter 63, Florida Statutes.

1. This is an action for adoption of a minor child(ren) by his or her (their) stepparent.

2. I desire to adopt the following child(ren):

	Name to be given to child(ren)	**Birth date**	**Birthplace**
a.			
b.			
c.			
d.			
e.			

A certified copy of the birth certificate(s) is/are attached.

3. The child(ren) has (have) resided with me since *{date}* ________________________________. I wish to adopt the child(ren) because I would like to legally establish the parent-child relationship already existing between the child(ren) and me. Since the above date, I have been able to provide adequately for the material needs of the child(ren) and am able to continue doing so in the future, as well as to provide for the child(ren)'s mental and emotional well-being. Other reasons I wish to adopt the children are:____
____
____
____
____
____

4. I am ______________ years old, and have resided at {street address}, ____ {city} _____________________ {county} __________ {state} _______ for _____________ years.

5. I married the _____ father or _____ mother of the child(ren) on *{date}* ____________________, in {city} _____________________ {county} __________ {state} _______. The following are the dates and places of my dissolutions of marriage, if any:

Date Place

a. ____

b. ____

6. A completed **Uniform Child Custody Jurisdiction and Enforcement Act Affidavit (UCCJEA)**, Florida Supreme Court Approved Family Law Form 12.902(d), is filed with this petition.

7. A description and estimate of the value of any property of the adoptee(s) is as follows:

____

____

____

____

8. Consent by the adoptee(s):

_____ is attached for: *Name(s)*

____

_____ is not required because the adoptee(s) is/are not 12 years of age: *Name(s)*

____

_____ was excused by the court for: *Name(s)*

____

9. The following person(s) is/are required to consent and the consent form or affidavit of nonpaternity is/are attached

____

10. The following person(s) whose consent is required has not consented. The facts/circumstances that excuse the lack of consent and would justify termination of this person's parental rights are:

Name Address Facts/circumstances

____

____

____

____

11. A copy of this Petition was served on all known persons whose consent is required but did not waive notice, as well as on all persons whose consent is

required but did not provide consent. Proof of service is attached.

{Indicate if applicable}:
_____ A search of the Putative Father Registry maintained by the Office of Vital Statistics of the Department of Health has been requested, and if granted, the certificate from the State Registrar will be filed in this action.

WHEREFORE, I request that this Court terminate the parental rights of ____________________________,

{name of parent whose rights are sought to be terminated}, enter a Final Judgment of Adoption of the Minor Child(ren) by Petitioner Stepparent and, as requested, change the name of the adoptee(s).

I understand that I am swearing or affirming under oath to the truthfulness of the claims made in this petition and that the punishment for knowingly making a false statement includes fines and/or imprisonment.

Dated: ______________________

____
Signature of Party
Printed Name:

____
Address:

____
__
City, State, Zip:

____
Telephone Number:

____
Fax Number:

____
Designated E-mail Address(es):

____

STATE OF FLORIDA
COUNTY OF ____________________

Sworn to or affirmed and signed before me on *{date}* ______________ .

____
NOTARY PUBLIC or DEPUTY CLERK

____
{Print, type, or stamp commissioned name of notary or deputy clerk.}

____ Personally known
____ Produced identification
Type of identification produced ______________________

IF A NONLAWYER HELPED YOU FILL OUT THIS FORM, HE/SHE MUST FILL IN THE BLANKS BELOW:
[fill in **all** blanks] This form was prepared for the: (   ) parent (   ) stepparent (   ) both .
This form was completed with the assistance of: *{name of individual}*
____,*{name of business}* ____,
*{address}*____
{city} ____________________, *{state}* _____, *{zip code}* _________, *{telephone number}*
_____________.

INSTRUCTIONS FOR FLORIDA SUPREME COURT APPROVED FAMILY LAW FORM 12.981(a)(1), STEPPARENT ADOPTION: CONSENT AND WAIVER BY PARENT (11/15)

When should this form be used?

This form is to be completed and signed by the parent who is giving up all rights to, custody of, and time-sharing with the minor child to be adopted. This consent shall not be executed before the birth of the minor child. For more information about consenting to adoption, you should refer to Chapter 63, Florida Statutes, and sections 63.062-63.082, Florida Statutes, in particular.

This form should be typed or printed in black ink. It must be signed in the presence of a **notary public** or **deputy clerk** and two witnesses other than the notary or clerk. You should **file** this form with the **Joint Petition for Adoption by Stepparent**, Florida Supreme Court Approved Family Law Form 12.981(b)(1).

After completing this form, you should hand deliver a copy or duplicate original to the parent giving consent and have them sign the original saying they received a copy. Then you should file the original with the **clerk of the circuit court** in the county where the **Joint Petition for Adoption by Stepparent**, Florida Supreme Court Approved Family Law Form 12.981(b)(1) is filed and keep a copy for your records.

IMPORTANT INFORMATION REGARDING E-FILING

The Florida Rules of Judicial Administration now require that all petitions, pleadings, and documents be filed electronically except in certain circumstances. **Self-represented litigants may file petitions or other pleadings or documents electronically; however, they are not required to do so.** If you choose to file your pleadings or other documents electronically, you must do so in accordance with Florida Rule of Judicial Administration 2.525, and you must follow the procedures of the judicial circuit in which you file. **The rules and procedures should be carefully read and followed.**

IMPORTANT INFORMATION REGARDING E-SERVICE ELECTION

After the initial service of process of the petition or supplemental petition by the Sheriff or certified process server, the Florida Rules of Judicial Administration now require that all documents required or permitted to be served on the other party must be served by electronic mail (e-mail) except in certain circumstances. **You must strictly comply with the format requirements set forth in the Rules of Judicial Administration.** If you elect to participate in electronic service, which means serving or receiving pleadings by electronic mail (e-mail), or through the Florida Courts E-Filing Portal, you **must** review Florida Rule of Judicial Administration 2.516. You may find this rule at www.flcourts.org through the link to the Rules of Judicial Administration provided under either Family Law Forms: Getting Started, or Rules of Court in the A-Z Topical Index.

SELF-REPRESENTED LITIGANTS MAY SERVE DOCUMENTS BY E-MAIL; HOWEVER, THEY ARE NOT REQUIRED TO DO SO. If a self-represented litigant elects to serve and receive documents by e-mail, the procedures must always be followed once the initial election is made.

To serve and receive documents by e-mail, you must designate your e-mail addresses by using the **Designation of Current Mailing and E-mail Address**, Florida Supreme Court Approved Family Law Form 12.915, and you must provide your e-mail address on each form on which your signature appears. Please

CAREFULLY read the rules and instructions for: **Certificate of Service (General),** Florida Supreme Court Approved Family Law Form 12.914; **Designation of Current Mailing and E-mail Address**, Florida Supreme Court Approved Family Law Form 12.915; and Florida Rule of Judicial Administration 2.516.

Special notes...

Remember, a person who is NOT an attorney is called a nonlawyer. If a nonlawyer helps you fill out these forms, that person must give you a copy of **Disclosure from Nonlawyer**, Florida Family Law Rules of Procedure Form 12.900 (a), before he or she helps you. A nonlawyer helping you fill out these forms also **must** put his or her name, address, and telephone number on the bottom of the last page of every form he or she helps you complete.

IN THE CIRCUIT COURT OF THE __________ JUDICIAL CIRCUIT,
IN AND FOR ________________________ COUNTY, FLORIDA

Case No.: ________________________
Division: ________________________

IN THE MATTER OF THE ADOPTION OF

____
{use name to be given to minor child(ren)} Adoptee(s).

CONSENT AND WAIVER BY PARENT

C) I, *{full legal name}* ______________________________, am the *{Choose only one}*
_____ father **or** _____ mother of the minor child(ren) subject to this consent who is/are:

	Child's Current Name	**Gender**	**Birth date**	**Birthplace** *{city, county, state}*
a.				
b.				
c.				
d.				
e.				
f.				

D) I relinquish all rights to, custody of, and time sharing with this (these) minor child(ren), *{name(s)}*
____,
with full knowledge of the legal effect of the stepparent adoption and consent to the adoption by the child(ren)'s stepparent whose name is: *{Choose only one}*
_____ *{name}* ____
_____ not required for my granting of this consent.

E) I understand my legal rights as a parent and I understand that I do not have to sign this consent and release of my parental rights. I acknowledge that this consent is being given knowingly, freely, and voluntarily. I further acknowledge that my consent is not given under fraud or duress. I understand that there is a "grace period" in Florida during which I may revoke my consent. If the child to be adopted is older than 6 months at the time of consent, this grace period is for 3 business days. The term "business day" means any day on which the United States Postal Service accepts certified mail for delivery. I understand that, in signing this consent, I am permanently and forever giving up all my parental rights to and interest in this (these) minor child(ren) and that this consent may only be withdrawn if the Court finds it was obtained by fraud or duress. I voluntarily, permanently relinquish all my parental rights to this (these) minor child(ren).

F) I consent, release, and give up permanently, of my own free will, my parental rights to this (these) minor child(ren), for the purpose of stepparent adoption.

G) I waive any further notice of the stepparent adoption proceeding.

H) I understand that pursuant to Chapter 63, Florida Statutes, "an action or proceeding of any kind to vacate, set aside, or otherwise nullify a judgment of adoption or an underlying judgment terminating parental rights on any ground may not be filed more than 1 year after entry of the judgment terminating parental rights."

I) I understand I have the right to choose a person who does not have an employment, professional, or personal relationship with the adoption entity or the prospective adoptive parents to be present when this affidavit is executed and to sign it as a witness. The witness I selected is: *{full legal name}*

____.

I understand that I am swearing or affirming under oath to the truthfulness of the claims made in this consent and waiver and that the punishment for knowingly making a false statement includes fines and/or imprisonment.

Dated: ______________________________

Signature of Parent:

____

Printed Name:

____

Address:

____

City, State, Zip:

____

Telephone Number:

____

Fax Number:

____

Designated E-mail Address(es):

____

____

____

Signature of Witness

Printed Name:

____

Business Address:

____

Home Address:

____

Driver's License No.:

____

State ID Card No.:

____

____

Signature of Witness

Printed Name:

____

Business Address:

____

Home Address:

____

Driver's License No.:

____

State ID Card No.:

____

STATE OF FLORIDA
COUNTY OF ____________________

Sworn to or affirmed and signed before me on *{date}* ______________ .

____
NOTARY PUBLIC or DEPUTY CLERK

____
{Print, type, or stamp commissioned name of notary or deputy clerk.}

____ Personally known
____ Produced identification
Type of identification produced ______________________

I hereby acknowledge receipt of a copy or duplicate original of this executed **Consent and Waiver**.

____
Signature of Parent

IF A NONLAWYER HELPED YOU FILL OUT THIS FORM, HE/SHE MUST FILL IN THE BLANKS BELOW:
[fill in **all** blanks] This form was prepared for the: *{choose only* ***one****}* ( ) Mother ( ) Father
This form was completed with the assistance of:
*{name of individual}*____,
*{name of business}*____,
*address}*____
{city} _______________,*{state}* _____, *{zip code}*_____________*{telephone number}*
_______________.

INSTRUCTIONS FOR FLORIDA SUPREME COURT APPROVED FAMILY LAW FORM 12.981(a)(2), STEPPARENT ADOPTION: CONSENT OF ADOPTEE (03/15)

When should this form be used?

This form must be completed and signed by the person being adopted, the adoptee, if he or she is **over 12 years of age**, unless the court, in the best interest of the minor excuses the minor's consent. It must be signed in the presence of a **notary public** or **deputy clerk** and two witnesses other than the notary public or deputy clerk.

This form should be typed or printed in black ink. After completing this form, you should **file** the original with the **clerk of the circuit court** in the county where the **Joint Petition for Adoption by Stepparent**, Florida Supreme Court Approved Family Law Form 12.981(b)(1) is filed and keep a copy for your records.

IMPORTANT INFORMATION REGARDING E-FILING

The Florida Rules of Judicial Administration now require that all petitions, pleadings, and documents be filed electronically except in certain circumstances. **Self-represented litigants may file petitions or other pleadings or documents electronically; however, they are not required to do so.** If you choose to file your pleadings or other documents electronically, you must do so in accordance with Florida Rule of Judicial Administration 2.525, and you must follow the procedures of the judicial circuit in which you file. **The rules and procedures should be carefully read and followed.**

Special notes...

Remember, a person who is NOT an attorney is called a nonlawyer. If a nonlawyer helps you fill out these forms, that person must give you a copy of **Disclosure from Nonlawyer**, Florida Family Law Rules of Procedure Form 12.900 (a), before he or she helps you. A nonlawyer helping you fill out these forms also **must** put his or her name, address, and telephone number on the bottom of the last page of every form he or she helps you complete.

IN THE CIRCUIT COURT OF THE _______ JUDICIAL CIRCUIT,
IN AND FOR _____________ COUNTY, FLORIDA

Case No.: ________________________
Division: ________________________

IN THE MATTER OF THE ADOPTION OF

____
{use name to be given to the child(ren)} Adoptee(s).

CONSENT OF ADOPTEE

1. I, *{full legal name}* __________________________________, being over the age of 12, consent to my adoption by *{name}* ____________________________, to be his/her legal child and heir at law.

2. I have been told of my right to choose a person who does not have an employment, professional, or personal relationship with the adoption entity or prospective adoptive parents to be present when this affidavit is executed and to sign it as a witness. The witness I selected is: *{full legal name}*____.

3. *{Choose only **one**]*

   ( ) I consent to my name being legally changed to *{specify}* ____________________.

   ( ) I do **not** consent to a name change.

I understand that I am swearing or affirming under oath to the truthfulness of the claims made in this consent and that the punishment for knowingly making a false statement includes fines and/or imprisonment.

Dated: ___________________

____
Signature of Adoptee
Printed Name: ___________________________
Address: _______________________________
City, State, Zip: ________________________
Telephone Number: ______________________
Fax Number: ____________________________
Designated E-mail Address(es):
____

____
Signature of Witness
Printed Name: __________________________
Business Address: ________________________
Home Address:__________________________
Driver's License No.: ______________________
State ID Card No.: ________________________

____
Signature of Witness
Printed Name: __________________________
Business Address: ________________________
Home Address:_______________________
Driver's License No.: ______________________
State ID Card No.: ________________________

STATE OF FLORIDA
COUNTY OF ___________________________

Sworn to or affirmed and signed before me on
{date} ___________________________________
.

____ -
NOTARY PUBLIC or DEPUTY CLERK

____
{Print, type, or stamp commissioned name of notary or deputy clerk.}

_____Personally known
_____Produced identification
Type of identification produced _____________________

IF A NONLAWYER HELPED YOU FILL OUT THIS FORM, HE/SHE MUST FILL IN THE BLANKS BELOW:
[fill in **all** blanks] This form was prepared for the *{choose only **one**}* ( ) adoptee ( ) stepparent
This form was completed with the assistance of:
*{name of individual}*____,
{name of business} ____,
{address} ____,
{city} _________________, *{state}* ______,*{zip code}*_________ *{telephone number}*
____________________.
.

INSTRUCTIONS FOR FLORIDA SUPREME COURT APPROVED FAMILY LAW FORM 12.981(a)(5), INDIAN CHILD WELFARE ACT AFFIDAVIT (11/15)

When should this form be used?

This form should be used in cases involving stepparent adoption of a child. This **affidavit** is **required**.

This form should be typed or printed in black ink. After completing this form, you should sign the form before a **notary public** or **deputy clerk**. You should then **file** the original with the **clerk of the circuit court** in the county where the petition was filed and keep a copy for your records.

IMPORTANT INFORMATION REGARDING E-FILING

The Florida Rules of Judicial Administration now require that all petitions, pleadings, and documents be filed electronically except in certain circumstances. **Self-represented litigants may file petitions or other pleading or documents electronically; however, they are not required to do so.** If you choose to file your pleadings or other documents electronically, you must do so in accordance with Florida Rule of Judicial Administration 2.525, and you must follow the procedures of the judicial circuit in which you file. **The rules and procedures should be carefully read and followed.**

What should I do next?

A copy of this form must be mailed, e-mailed, or hand delivered to the other party in your case, if it is not served on him or her with your initial papers.

IMPORTANT INFORMATION REGARDING E-SERVICE ELECTION

After the initial service of process of the petition or supplemental petition by the Sheriff or certified process server, the Florida Rules of Judicial Administration now require that all documents required or permitted to be served on the other party must be served by electronic mail (e-mail) except in certain circumstances. **You must strictly comply with the format requirements set forth in the Rules of Judicial Administration.** If you elect to participate in electronic service, which means serving or receiving pleadings by electronic mail (e-mail), or through the Florida Courts E-Filing Portal, you **must** review Florida Rule of Judicial Administration 2.516. You may find this rule at www.flcourts.org through the link to the Rules of Judicial Administration provided under either Family Law Forms: Getting Started, or Rules of Court in the A-Z Topical Index.

SELF-REPRESENTED LITIGANTS MAY SERVE DOCUMENTS BY E-MAIL; HOWEVER, THEY ARE NOT REQUIRED TO DO SO. If a self-represented litigant elects to serve and receive documents by e-mail, the procedures must always be followed once the initial election is made.

To serve and receive documents by e-mail, you must designate your e-mail addresses by using the **Designation of Current Mailing and E-mail Address**, Florida Supreme Court Approved Family Law Form 12.915, and you must provide your e-mail address on each form on which your signature appears. Please **CAREFULLY** read the rules and instructions for: **Certificate of Service (General),** Florida Supreme Court Approved Family Law Form 12.914; **Designation of Current Mailing and E-mail Address**, Florida Supreme Court Approved Family Law Form 12.915; and Florida Rule of Judicial Administration 2.516.

Where can I look for more information?

Before proceeding, you should read General Information for Self-Represented Litigants found at the beginning of these forms. The words that are in **bold underline** in these instructions are defined there.

Special notes...

Remember, a person who is NOT an attorney is called a nonlawyer. If a nonlawyer helps you fill out these forms, that person must give you a copy of a **Disclosure from Nonlawyer**, Florida Family Law Rules of Procedure Form 12.900 (a), before he or she helps you. A nonlawyer helping you fill out these forms also **must** put his or her name, address, and telephone number on the bottom of the last page of every form he or she helps you complete.

IN THE CIRCUIT COURT OF THE _________________ JUDICIAL CIRCUIT,
IN AND FOR ________________________ COUNTY, FLORIDA

Case No.:
____
Division:
____

IN THE MATTER OF THE ADOPTION OF

____,
{use name to be given to the minor child(ren)} Adoptee(s).

INDIAN CHILD WELFARE ACT AFFIDAVIT

I, *{full legal name}* ____________________________________, being sworn, certify that the following statements are true:

Upon information and belief the child ___________________________________ *{name}* subject to this proceeding*: {choose **one** only}*

b. _____ is not an Indian child. The Indian Child Welfare Act does not apply to this proceeding.

c. _____ is an Indian child within the meaning of the Indian Child Welfare Act of 1978 (25 U.S.C. Section 1901 et seq.).

I certify that a copy of this document was ( ) mailed ( ) faxed and mailed ( ) e-mailed ( ) hand-delivered to the person(s) listed below on *{date}* ____________________.

Other party or his/her attorney:
Name: ___________________________________
Address: _________________________________
City, State, Zip:_______________________________
Fax Number: ______________________________
Designated E-mail Address(es): _______________
____

I understand that I am swearing or affirming under oath to the truthfulness of the claims made in this affidavit and that the punishment for knowingly making a false statement includes fines and/or imprisonment.

Dated: ____________________

____
Signature of Party
Printed Name: __________________
Address: ______________________
City, State, Zip: ________________
Telephone Number: _____________

Fax Number: _________________
Designated E-mail Address(es):
____

STATE OF FLORIDA
COUNTY OF ________________

Sworn to or affirmed and signed before me on *{date}* ____________ .

_________________________________ -
NOTARY PUBLIC or DEPUTY CLERK

____
{Print, type, or stamp commissioned name of notary or deputy clerk.}

_____Personally known
_____Produced identification
Type of identification produced ________________

IF A NONLAWYER HELPED YOU FILL OUT THIS FORM, HE/SHE MUST FILL IN THE BLANKS BELOW:
[fill in **all** blanks] This form was prepared for the: *{choose only **one**}* ( ) Petitioner ( ) Respondent
This form was completed with the assistance of:
{name of individual} ____,
{name of business} ____,
{address} ____,
{city} ___________________, *{state}* _____, *{zip code}* _________, *{telephone number}* ___________.

INSTRUCTIONS FOR FLORIDA SUPREME COURT APPROVED FAMILY LAW FORM 12.902(d) UNIFORM CHILD CUSTODY JURISDICTION AND ENFORCEMENT ACT (UCCJEA) AFFIDAVIT (11/15)

When should this form be used?

This form should be used in any case involving custody of, visitation with, or time-sharing with any minor child(ren). This **affidavit** is **required** even if the custody of, visitation, or time-sharing with the minor child(ren) are not in dispute.

This form should be typed or printed in black ink. After completing this form, you should sign the form before a **notary public** or **deputy clerk**. You should then **file** the original with the **clerk of the circuit court** in the county where the petition was filed and keep a copy for your records.

IMPORTANT INFORMATION REGARDING E-FILING

The Florida Rules of Judicial Administration now require that all petitions, pleadings, and documents be filed electronically except in certain circumstances. **Self-represented litigants may file petitions or other pleadings or documents electronically; however, they are not required to do so.** If you choose to file your pleadings or other documents electronically, you must do so in accordance with Florida Rule of Judicial Administration 2.525, and you must follow the procedures of the judicial circuit in which you file. **The rules and procedures should be carefully read and followed.**

What should I do next?

A copy of this form must be mailed, e-mailed, or hand delivered to the other party in your case, if it is not served on him or her with your initial papers.

IMPORTANT INFORMATION REGARDING E-SERVICE ELECTION

After the initial service of process of the petition or supplemental petition by the Sheriff or certified process server, the Florida Rules of Judicial Administration now require that all documents required or permitted to be served on the other party must be served by electronic mail (e-mail) except in certain circumstances. **You must strictly comply with the format requirements set forth in the Rules of Judicial Administration**. If you elect to participate in electronic service, which means serving or receiving pleadings by electronic mail (e-mail), or through the Florida Courts E-Filing Portal, you **must** review Florida Rule of Judicial Administration 2.516. You may find this rule at www.flcourts.org through the link to the Rules of Judicial Administration provided under either Family Law Forms: Getting Started, or Rules of Court in the A-Z Topical Index.

SELF-REPRESENTED LITIGANTS MAY SERVE DOCUMENTS BY E-MAIL; HOWEVER, THEY ARE NOT REQUIRED TO DO SO. If a self-represented litigant elects to serve and receive documents by e-mail, the procedures must always be followed once the initial election is made.

To serve and receive documents by e-mail, you must designate your e-mail addresses by using the **Designation**

of Current Mailing and E-mail Address, Florida Supreme Court Approved Family Law Form 12.915, and you must provide your e-mail address on each form on which your signature appears. Please CAREFULLY read the rules and instructions for: **Certificate of Service (General)**, Florida Supreme Court Approved Family Law Form 12.914**; Designation of Current Mailing and E-mail Address**, Florida Supreme Court Approved Family Law Form 12.915; and Florida Rule of Judicial Administration 2.516.

Where can I look for more information?

Before proceeding, you should read General Information for Self-Represented Litigants found at the beginning of these forms. The words that are in **bold underline** in these instructions are defined there. For further information, see sections 61.501-61.542, Florida Statutes.

Special notes...

Chapter 2008-61, Laws of Florida, effective October 1, 2008, eliminated such terms as custodial parent, noncustodial parent, primary residential parent, secondary residential parent, and visitation from Chapter 61, Florida Statutes. Instead, parents are to develop a Parenting Plan that includes, among other things, their time-sharing schedule with the minor child(ren). If the parents cannot agree, a parenting plan will be established by the Court. However, because the UCCJEA uses the terms custody and visitation, they are included in this form.

If you are the petitioner in an injunction for protection against domestic violence case and you have filed a **Request for Confidential Filing of Address**, Florida Supreme Court Approved Family Law Form 12.980(h), you should write confidential in any space on this form that would require you to write the address where you are currently living.

Remember, a person who is NOT an attorney is called a nonlawyer. If a nonlawyer helps you fill out these forms, that person must give you a copy of a **Disclosure from Nonlawyer**, Florida Family Law Rules of Procedure Form 12.900(a), before he or she helps you. A nonlawyer helping you fill out these forms also **must** put his or her name, address, and telephone number on the bottom of the last page of every form he or she helps you complete.

IN THE CIRCUIT COURT OF THE______________________JUDICIAL CIRCUIT,
IN AND FOR______________________COUNTY, FLORIDA

Case No.:______________________
__
Division:______________________
____

______________________________,
Petitioner,

and

______________________________,
Respondent.

UNIFORM CHILD CUSTODY JURISDICTION AND ENFORCEMENT ACT (UCCJEA) AFFIDAVIT

I, {full legal name} ______________________________, being sworn, certify that the following statements are true:

The number of minor child(ren) subject to this proceeding is _________. The name, place of birth, birth date, and sex of each child; the present address, periods of residence, and places where each child has lived **within the past five (5) years**; and the name, present address, and relationship to the child of each person with whom the child has lived during that time are:

THE FOLLOWING INFORMATION IS TRUE ABOUT CHILD #__1__:

Child's Full Legal Name: ______________________________
Place of Birth: ______________ Date of Birth: ________________ Sex: ________________

Child's Residence for the past 5 years:

Dates (From/To)	Address (including city and state) where child lived	Name and present address of person child lived with	Relationship to child
_____/present*			
____/____			
____/____			
____/____			
____/____			

____/____			

*** If you are the petitioner in an injunction for protection against domestic violence case and you have filed a Request for Confidential Filing of Address, Florida Supreme Court Approved Family Law Form 12.980(h), you should write confidential in any space on this form that would require you to enter the address where you are currently living.**

THE FOLLOWING INFORMATION IS TRUE ABOUT CHILD # ______:

Child's Full Legal Name: ____
Place of Birth: __________________ Date of Birth: __________________ Sex: _________________

Child's Residence for the past 5 years:

Dates (From/To)	Address (including city and state) where child lived	Name and present address of person child lived with	Relationship to child
_____/present*			
____/____			
____/____			
____/____			
____/____			
____/____			

THE FOLLOWING INFORMATION IS TRUE ABOUT CHILD # ______:

Child's Full Legal Name:
____
Place of Birth: __________________ Date of Birth: __________________ Sex: _________________

Child's Residence for the past 5 years:

Dates (From/To)	Address (including city and state) where child lived	Name and present address of person child lived with	Relationship to child
____/present*			
___/___			
___/___			
___/___			
___/___			
___/___			

2. **Participation in custody or time-sharing proceeding(s):**
*[Choose only **one**]*

____ I HAVE NOT participated as a party, witness, or in any capacity in any other litigation or custody proceeding in this or any other state, concerning custody of or time-sharing with a child subject to this proceeding.

____ I HAVE participated as a party, witness, or in any capacity in any other litigation or custody proceeding in this or another state, concerning custody of or time-sharing with a child subject to this proceeding. *Explain*:

a. Name of each child:

____

b. Type of proceeding:

____

c. Court and state:

____

d. Date of court order or judgment (if any):

____

3. **Information about custody or time-sharing proceeding(s):**
*[Choose only **one**]*

____ I HAVE NO INFORMATION of any custody or time-sharing proceeding pending in a court of this or any other state concerning a child subject to this proceeding.

____ I HAVE THE FOLLOWING INFORMATION concerning a custody or time-sharing proceeding pending in a court of this or another state concerning a child subject to this proceeding, other than set out in item 2. *Explain:*

e. Name of each child:

____

f. Type of proceeding:

____

g. Court and state:

____

h. Date of court order or judgment (if any):

____

4. Persons not a party to this proceeding:

*[Choose only **one**]*

____ I DO NOT KNOW OF ANY PERSON not a party to this proceeding who has physical custody or claims to have custody, visitation or time-sharing with respect to any child subject to this proceeding.

____ I KNOW THAT THE FOLLOWING NAMED PERSON(S) not a party to this proceeding has (have) physical custody or claim(s) to have custody, visitation, or time-sharing with respect to any child subject to this proceeding:

a. Name and address of person:

____

____

______

_____ has physical custody _____ claims custody rights _____ claims visitation or time-sharing

Name of each child:

b. Name and address of person:

____

____

______

_____ has physical custody _____ claims custody rights _____ claims visitation or time-sharing

Name of each child: ____

____

______

c. Name and address of person:

____

____

______

_____ has physical custody _____ claims custody rights _____claims visitation or time-sharing

Name of each child: ____

____

______

5. Knowledge of prior child support proceedings:

*[Choose only **one**]*

_____The child(ren) described in this affidavit are NOT subject to existing child support order(s) in this or any state or territory.

_____The child(ren) described in this affidavit are subject to the following existing child support

order(s):
Name of each child:

____

Type of proceeding:

____

Court and address:

____

Date of court order/judgment (if any):

____

Amount of child support paid and by whom:

____

6. **I acknowledge that I have a continuing duty to advise this Court of any custody, visitation or time-sharing, child support, or guardianship proceeding (including dissolution of marriage, separate maintenance, child neglect, or dependency) concerning the child(ren) in this state or any other state about which information is obtained during this proceeding.**

I certify that a copy of this document was ( ) mailed ( ) faxed and mailed ( ) e-mailed ( ) hand delivered to the person(s) listed below on {date}

____.

Other party or his/her attorney:
Name: ___________________________________
Address: _________________________________
City, State, Zip: ____________________________
Fax Number: ________________________________
Designated E-mail Address(es):__________________

____

I understand that I am swearing or affirming under oath to the truthfulness of the claims made in this petition and that the punishment for knowingly making a false statement includes fines and/or imprisonment.

Dated: ______________________ ____

Signature of _____ HUSBAND _____ WIFE

Printed Name: ________________________________
Address: ____________________________________
City, State, Zip: _____________________________
Telephone Number: ____________________________
Fax Number: _________________________________
Designated E-mail Address(es): ___________________

STATE OF FLORIDA
COUNTY OF ____________________

Sworn to or affirmed and signed before me on ____________ by ______________________________.

____
NOTARY PUBLIC or DEPUTY CLERK

____
{Print, type, or stamp commissioned name of notary or deputy clerk.}

_____ Personally known
_____ Produced identification
Type of identification produced ______________________________

IF A NONLAWYER HELPED YOU FILL OUT THIS FORM, HE/SHE MUST FILL IN THE BLANKS BELOW:
[fill in all blanks] This form was prepared for the: *{choose only* ***one****}* ( ) Husband ( ) Wife
This form was completed with the assistance of:
{name of individual} ____,
{name of business} ____,
{address} ____,
{city} ______________,*{state}* _____,*{zip code}*__________,*{telephone number}* _______________.

INSTRUCTIONS FOR FLORIDA SUPREME COURT APPROVED FAMILY LAW FORM 12.981(a)(6), MOTION FOR SEARCH OF THE PUTATIVE FATHER REGISTRY (11/15)

When should this form be used?

This form should be used when a stepparent is adopting his or her **spouse's** child. Section 63.054, Florida Statutes, requires that a search of Florida's Putative Father Registry be conducted in every adoption proceeding. The Office of Vital Statistics of the Department of Health has an application available called Florida Putative Father Registry - Application for Search which should be completed and attached to this form. The Office of Vital Statistics is allowed to charge for searching the registry. You may wish to contact that office in advance to find out what amount and method of payment will be accepted.

This form should be typed or printed in black ink. The name to be given to the adoptee **after** the adoption should be used in the heading of the **petition**. The stepparent is the **petitioner**, because he or she is the one who is asking the court for legal action. You must have your signature witnessed by a **notary public** or **deputy clerk**.

After completing this form, you should **file** the original with the **clerk of the circuit court** in the county where you have filed the **Joint Petition for Adoption by Stepparent,** Florida Supreme Court Approved Family Law Form 12.981(b)(1) and keep a copy for your records. These family law forms contain an **Order Granting Motion for Search of Putative Father Registry,** Florida Supreme Court Approved Family Law Form 12.981(a)(7), which the judge may use. You should check with the clerk, family law intake staff or judicial assistant to see if you need to provide this form order to the judge with your motion. If so, you should type or print the heading, including the circuit, county, case number, division, and the child(ren)'s name, and leave the rest blank for the judge to complete.

IMPORTANT INFORMATION REGARDING E-FILING

The Florida Rules of Judicial Administration now require that all petitions, pleadings, and documents be filed electronically except in certain circumstances. **Self-represented litigants may file petitions or other pleadings or documents electronically; however, they are not required to do so.** If you choose to file your pleadings or other documents electronically, you must do so in accordance with Florida Rule of Judicial Administration 2.525, and you must follow the procedures of the judicial circuit in which you file. **The rules and procedures should be carefully read and followed.**

What should I do next?

If the judge grants your motion, you will need to take the order, your completed application, and any fee to the Office of Vital Statistics. That office will conduct the search and file the results with the clerk of court. You may call the clerk's office to determine when the results have been filed in order to set a final hearing.

Where can I look for more information?

Before proceeding, you should read General Information for Self-Represented Litigants found at the beginning of these forms. See Chapter 63, Florida Statutes, and Florida Family Law Rule 12.200(a)(2) for further information.

IMPORTANT INFORMATION REGARDING E-SERVICE ELECTION

After the initial service of process of the petition or supplemental petition by the Sheriff or certified process server, the Florida Rules of Judicial Administration now require that all documents required or permitted to be served on the other party must be served by electronic mail (e-mail) except in certain circumstances. **You must strictly comply with the format requirements set forth in the Rules of Judicial Administration.** If you elect to participate in electronic service, which means serving or receiving pleadings by electronic mail (e-mail), or through the Florida Courts E-Filing Portal, you **must** review Florida Rule of Judicial Administration 2.516. You may find this rule at www.flcourts.org through the link to the Rules of Judicial Administration provided under either Family Law Forms: Getting Started, or Rules of Court in the A-Z Topical Index.

SELF-REPRESENTED LITIGANTS MAY SERVE DOCUMENTS BY E-MAIL; HOWEVER, THEY ARE NOT REQUIRED TO DO SO. If a self-represented litigant elects to serve and receive documents by e-mail, the procedures must always be followed once the initial election is made.

To serve and receive documents by e-mail, you must designate your e-mail addresses by using the **Designation of Current Mailing and E-mail Address**, Florida Supreme Court Approved Family Law Form 12.915, and you must provide your e-mail address on each form on which your signature appears. Please **CAREFULLY** read the rules and instructions for: **Certificate of Service (General),** Florida Supreme Court Approved Family Law Form 12.914; **Designation of Current Mailing and E-mail Address**, Florida Supreme Court Approved Family Law Form 12.915; and Florida Rule of Judicial Administration 2.516.

Special notes...

THIS ADOPTION MAY AFFECT THE ADOPTEE'S INHERITANCE.

Remember, a person who is NOT an attorney is called a nonlawyer. If a nonlawyer helps you fill out these forms, that person must give you a copy of a **Disclosure from Nonlawyer**, Florida Family Law Rules of Procedure Form 12.900 (a), before he or she helps you. A nonlawyer helping you fill out these forms also **must** put his or her name, address, and telephone number on the bottom of the last page of every form he or she helps you complete.

IN THE CIRCUIT COURT OF THE ________________ JUDICIAL CIRCUIT,
IN AND FOR ________________ COUNTY, FLORIDA

Case No.: ______________________

Division: ______________________

IN THE MATTER OF THE ADOPTION OF

______________________________________,
{use name to be given to the minor child} Adoptee.

MOTION FOR SEARCH OF THE PUTATIVE FATHER REGISTRY

Petitioner, *{full legal name}* ____________________________________, files this Motion for Search of the Putative Father Registry, pursuant to Chapter 63, Florida Statutes, and states:

d. This is an action for adoption of a minor by the child's stepparent, who is the Petitioner. .

e. Section 63.054, Florida Statutes, requires that in every adoption, a search of the Putative Father Registry maintained by the Department of Health, Office of Vital Statistics be conducted. Section 63.0541, Florida Statutes, makes information maintained by the Registry confidential and exempt from public disclosure, except that it may be disclosed to adoption entities, registrant unmarried biological fathers, and the court, upon issuance of a court order concerning a petitioner acting pro se.

f. The Florida Putative Father Registry - Application for Search is completed and attached to this Motion.

WHEREFORE, I request that this Court enter an Order Granting Motion for Search of the Putative Father Registry.

I understand that I am swearing or affirming under oath to the truthfulness of the claims made in this motion and that the punishment for knowingly making a false statement includes fines and/or imprisonment.

Dated: ____________________

____
Signature of Party
Printed Name:
____
Address:
____
City, State, Zip:
____
Telephone Number:
____
Fax Number:
____
Designated E-mail Address(es):
____
____

STATE OF FLORIDA
COUNTY OF ____________________

Sworn to or affirmed and signed before me on __________ by ______________________________.

____
NOTARY PUBLIC or DEPUTY CLERK

____
{Print, type, or stamp commissioned name of notary or deputy clerk.}

_____ Personally known
_____ Produced identification
Type of identification produced ______________________________

IF A NONLAWYER HELPED YOU FILL OUT THIS FORM, HE/SHE MUST FILL IN THE BLANKS BELOW:
[fill in **all** blanks] This form was prepared for the petitioner.
This form was completed with the assistance of:
{name of individual} ____,
{name of business} ____,

{address} ____,
{city} ____________________, *{state}* _____, *{zip code}* __________, *{telephone number}*
_____________.

IN THE CIRCUIT COURT OF THE ________________ JUDICIAL CIRCUIT,
IN AND FOR ______________________________ COUNTY, FLORIDA

Case No.: ____________________________
Division: ____________________________

IN THE MATTER OF THE ADOPTION OF

____,
{use name to be given to the minor child} Adoptee.

ORDER GRANTING MOTION FOR SEARCH OF THE PUTATIVE FATHER REGISTRY

Upon consideration of Petitioner's Motion for Search of the Putative Father Registry, this Court finds:

1. This is an action for adoption of a minor by the child's stepparent, Petitioner, who is proceeding pro se.

2. Section 63.054, Florida Statutes, requires that in every adoption, a search of the Putative Father Registry maintained by the Department of Health, Office of Vital Statistics be conducted. Section 63.0541, Florida Statutes, makes information maintained by the Registry confidential and exempt, except that it may be disclosed to adoption entities, registrant unmarried biological fathers, the birth mother, and the court, upon issuance of a court order concerning a petitioner acting pro se.

NOW, THEREFORE, IT IS ORDERED THAT:

1. The Office of Vital Statistics, Department of Health shall conduct a search of the Putative Father Registry upon receipt of a completed application and payment of any authorized fee.

2. The State Registrar shall issue a certificate indicating the results of such search which shall be filed in this proceeding by transmitting the certificate to the clerk of court.

DONE and ORDERED on: ____________________ in ___________________________, Florida.

____
Circuit Judge

I certify that a copy of the *{name of document(s)}* ____
was ( ) mailed ( ) faxed and mailed ( ) e-mailed ( ) hand-delivered to the parties and to any other persons or entities listed below on *{date}* ____.

____
By: Clerk of Court, Designee, or Judicial Assistant

Petitioner (or his or her attorney)
Other: _______________________
State Registrar, Office of Vital Statistics

THE CIRCUIT COURT OF THE _________ JUDICIAL CIRCUIT,
IN AND FOR _________________________ COUNTY, FLORIDA

Case No.: __________________________
Division: ___________________________

IN THE MATTER OF THE ADOPTION OF

_______________________________________,
{use name to be given to child(ren)} Adoptee(s).

FINAL JUDGMENT OF STEPPARENT ADOPTION

Upon consideration of the Joint Petition for Adoption by Stepparent and the evidence presented, the Court finds that:

J) The Court has subject matter jurisdiction over the Joint Petition for Adoption by Stepparent.

K) The Court has jurisdiction over the minor child(ren) subject to the Joint Petition for Adoption by Stepparent.

L) Petitioner desires the permanent responsibility of a parent in this adoption.

M) There is no pending litigation regarding the child(ren) in Florida or in any other state, nor is there any other person not a party to these proceedings who has or claims to have physical custody or rights to the minor child(ren).

N) The consent of the birth _____mother _____ father who is not married to Petitioner is:
*{Choose only **one**}*
_____ Attached to the petition
_____ Not required because he or she is deceased. A certified copy of the death certificate is attached.
_____ Waived because:
[Indicate all that apply]
_____ The parent has deserted the child without means of identification or has abandoned the child.
_____ The parent's rights have been terminated by a court of competent jurisdiction.
_____ The parent has been declared incompetent and restoration of competency is medically improbable.
_____ The legal guardian or lawful custodian of the adoptee(s), other than the birth parent, who has failed to respond in writing to a request for consent for a period of 60 days or the Court has examined the written reasons for withholding consent and has found the withholding of consent to be unreasonable.
_____ Other: ____.

O) The best interests of the child(ren) will be promoted by this adoption.

P) The minor child(ren) is (are) suitable for adoption by Petitioner.

NOW, THEREFORE, IT IS ORDERED that:

D) The minor child(ren) subject to the Petition is (are) declared to be the legal child(ren) of Petitioner,____ *{name}*

E) The minor child(ren) shall be the child(ren) and legal heir(s) at law of Petitioner, ____, *{name}*

and shall be entitled to all rights and privileges, and subject to all obligations, of child(ren) born of Petitioner.

F) All legal relations between the adoptee(s) and the parent whose rights are being terminated and between the adoptee(s) and the relatives of that parent are terminated by this adoption, as are all parental rights and responsibilities of that birth parent.

G) This Final Judgment of Adoption creates a relationship between the adoptee(s) and Petitioner and all relatives of Petitioner that would have existed if the adoptee(s) was (were) a blood descendant of the Petitioner, born within wedlock, entitled to all rights and privileges thereof, and subject to all obligations of a child being born to Petitioner.

H) The minor child(ren) shall hereafter be known as *{full legal name(s)}*:

____
____
____
____

DONE AND ORDERED at ______________________________, Florida on ____________________.

____
CIRCUIT JUDGE

I certify that a copy of *{name of document(s)}* ______________________________________was ( ) mailed ( ) faxed and mailed ( ) e-mailed ( ) hand-delivered to the parties and any persons or entities listed below on *{date}* ____________________________________.

____
By: Clerk of Court, Designee, or Judicial Assistant

Petitioners (or their attorney)
Other: ______________________________

APPENDIX II - OTHER FAMILY ADOPTION FORMS

The following forms are to be used in conjunction with the forms in the Required Forms set. These forms are slightly different as they are set up for family adoptions other than stepparent adoptions. These are not Florida Supreme Court approved forms. Some circuits use these forms or similar forms as local forms. There are no statewide Florida Supreme Court approved forms for any type of Florida family adoption, except for stepparent adoption.

IN THE CIRCUIT COURT OF THE __________________ JUDICIAL CIRCUIT,
IN AND FOR __________________ COUNTY, FLORIDA

Case No.:
Division:

IN THE MATTER OF THE TERMINATION OF PARENTAL RIGHTS FOR THE PROPOSED ADOPTION OF MINOR CHILD:

____

CONSENT AND WAIVER BY PARENT

1. I, ______________________________, am the ( )father ( ) mother of the minor child subject to this consent who is/ are:

____

2. I relinquish all rights to, custody of, and time sharing with the minor child(ren), __________________________________, with full knowledge of the legal effect of this adoption and consent to the adoption by the child's relatives whose name are:

__________________________; and ________________________________; and who

are related to the child as: ______________________________

3. I understand my legal rights as a parent and I understand that I do not have to sign this consent and release of my parental rights. I acknowledge that this consent is being given knowingly; freely, and voluntarily. I further acknowledge that my consent is not given under fraud or duress. I understand that there is a "grace period" in Florida during which I may revoke my consent. If the child to be adopted is older than 6 months at the time of consent, this grace period is for 3 days or until the child has been placed with the prospective adoptive parents, whichever is later. I understand that in signing this consent, I am permanently and forever giving up all my parental rights to and interest in this/these minor child(ren) and that this consent may only be withdrawn if the Court finds it was obtained by fraud or duress. I voluntarily, permanently relinquish all my parental rights to this/these minor child(ren).

4. I consent, release, and give up permanently, of my own free will, my parental rights to this/these minor child(ren), for the purpose of this family adoption.

5. I waive any further notice of the adoption proceeding.

6. I understand that pursuant to Chapter 63, Florida Statutes, "an action or proceeding of any kind to vacate, set aside, or otherwise nullify a judgment of adoption or an underlying judgment terminating

parental rights may not be filed more than 1 year after entry of the judgment terminating parental rights."

7. I understand I have the right to choose a person who does not have an employment, professional, or personal relations with the adoption entity or the prospective adoptive parents to be present when this affidavit is executed and to sign it as a witness. The witness selected is:

____.

I understand that I am swearing or affirming under oath to the truthfulness of the claims made in this petition and that the punishment for knowingly making a false statement includes fines and/or imprisonment.

Dated: ________________________

____
Signature of Parent
Name: ____________________________
Address: __________________________
City, State, Zip: ______________________
Telephone Number: ____________________
Fax Number:_________________________

______________________________	______________________________
Signature of Witness	Signature of Witness
Printed Name: ____________________	Printed Name: ____________________
Business Address: _________________	Business Address: _________________
Home Address:____________________	Home Address:____________________
Driver's License No.: ______________	Driver's License No.: ______________
State ID Card No.: ________________	State ID Card No.: ________________

STATE OF FLORIDA COUNTY OF________________________
Sworn to or affirmed and signed before me on __________________by ___________
______________________________________ .

NOTARY PUBLIC or DEPUTY CLERK

____
[Print, type, or stamp commissioned name of notary or deputy clerk.]

_____ Personally known
_____ Produced identification
Type of identification produced ______________________________

IF A NONLAWYER HELPED YOU FILL OUT THIS FORM, HE/SHE MUST FILL IN THE BLANKS BELOW: [Nfill in **all** blanks]
I, *{full legal name and trade name of nonlawyer}* ______________________________,
a nonlawyer, located at *{street}* ______________________________, *{city}* ______________,
{state} ____________, *{phone}* ________________, helped *{name}* ______________________,
who is the [/ **one** only] ___ petitioner **or** ___ respondent, fill out this form.

IN THE CIRCUIT COURT OF THE ______________________ JUDICIAL CIRCUIT,
IN AND FOR ______________________COUNTY, FLORIDA

CASE NO.____________

IN THE MATTER OF THE TERMINATION OF PARENTAL RIGHTS FOR THE PROPOSED ADOPTION OF MINOR CHILD:

______________________________.

JOINT PETITION FOR ADOPTION BY RELATIVE(S)

Petitioners. ____________________, and ________________________, being sworn, file this petition for adoption of the above-named minor child, under chapter 63, Florida Statutes.

1. This is an action for adoption of a minor children by the child's ______________________.

2. We desire to adopt the following child:

____

Name to be given to child: ______________________________
Birth date: ____________________________
Birthplace: ___________________________

A certified copy of the child's birth certificate is attached.

3. The child, _____________________ has resided with us since ________________.

We wish to adopt the child because to legally establish the parent-child relationship already existing between the child and us. Since the above date, we have been able to provide adequately for the material needs of the child and are able to continue doing so in the future, as well as to provide for the child's mental and emotional well-being. Other reasons we wish to adopt the child are:

____
____
____
____

4. I, ______________________________, Petitioner and the child's __________________ am years old. I have resided at: ____, for ____________________

5. I, ______________________________, Petitioner and the child's __________________ am ___ years old. I have resided at: ____, for ____________________.

6. A completed **Uniform Child Custody Jurisdiction and Enforcement Act Affidavit (UCCJEA)**, Florida Supreme Court Approved Family Law Form 12.902(d), is filed with this petition.

7. A description and estimate of the value of any property of the adoptee is as follows:

____

.

8. ____ Consent by the adoptee is not required because the adoptee is not 12 years of age.
____ Consent by the adoptee is attached hereto.

9. The following persons are required to consent and the consent forms are attached:

____, mother of the minor child consents to this adoption.

____, father of the minor child consents to this adoption.

____, mother of the minor children was never married to the

father of ____.

The minor child's mother, __________________________ was not married to anyone at the time of the child's birth or conception.

10. The following person whose consent may be required has not consented. The facts/circumstances that excuse the lack of consent and would justify termination of parental rights are as follows:

____
____
____

WHEREFORE, we request that this Court terminate the parental rights of __________________, and ______________________________________; and enter a Final Judgment of Adoption of the Minor Child by Petitioners.

I understand that I am swearing or affirming under oath to the truthfulness of the claims made in this petition and that the punishment for knowingly making a false statement includes fines and/or imprisonment.

Dated: ______________________

____

Signature of Petitioner,

Address: ___________________________
City, State, Zip: _____________________
Telephone Number: ___________________
Fax Number: ____________________________

STATE OF FLORIDA
COUNTY OF______________________

Sworn to or affirmed and signed before me on _________________by .
NOTARY PUBLIC or DEPUTY CLERK ____ .
[Print, type, or stamp commissioned name of notary or deputy clerk.] _____ Personally known _____
Produced identification
Type of identification produced ____________________________

I understand that I am swearing or affirming under oath to the truthfulness of the claims made in this petition and that the punishment for knowingly making a false statement includes fines and/or imprisonment.

Dated: ______________________

____

Signature of Petitioner,

Address: ___________________________
City, State, Zip: _____________________
Telephone Number: ___________________
Fax Number: ____________________________

STATE OF FLORIDA
COUNTY OF_______________________

Sworn to or affirmed and signed before me on _________________by .
NOTARY PUBLIC or DEPUTY CLERK ____
[Print, type, or stamp commissioned name of notary or deputy clerk.]
_____ Personally known
_____ Produced identification
Type of identification produced ____________________________

IF A NONLAWYER HELPED YOU FILL OUT THIS FORM, HE/SHE MUST FILL IN THE BLANKS BELOW: [Nfill in **all** blanks]
I, *{full legal name and trade name of nonlawyer}* ____________________________________,
a nonlawyer, located at *{street}* ___________________________, *{city}* ____________________,
{state} ___________, *{phone}* _______________, helped *{name}* ______________________,
who is the [/ **one** only] ___ petitioner **or** ___ respondent, fill out this form.

IN THE CIRCUIT COURT OF THE ______________________ JUDICIAL CIRCUIT,
IN AND FOR ______________________COUNTY, FLORIDA

CASE NO.____________

IN THE MATTER OF THE TERMINATION OF PARENTAL RIGHTS FOR THE PROPOSED ADOPTION OF MINOR CHILD:

____________________________________.

PETITION FOR ADOPTION BY RELATIVE

Petitioner. ______________________. being sworn, file this petition for adoption of the above-named minor child, under chapter 63, Florida Statutes.

1. This is an action for adoption of a minor children by the child's ______________________.

2. I desire to adopt the following child:

____

Name to be given to child: ________________________________
Birth date: ________________________________
Birthplace: ______________________________

A certified copy of the child's birth certificate is attached.

3. The child, ______________________ has resided with me since __________________.

I wish to adopt the child because to legally establish the parent-child relationship already existing between the child and me. Since the above date, I have been able to provide adequately for the material needs of the child and am able to continue doing so in the future, as well as to provide for the child's mental and emotional well-being. Other reasons I wish to adopt the child are:

____
____
____
____

4. I, ________________________________, Petitioner and the child's ____________________ am years old. I have resided at: ____, for ____________________

5. A completed **Uniform Child Custody Jurisdiction and Enforcement Act Affidavit (UCCJEA)**, Florida Supreme Court Approved Family Law Form 12.902(d), is filed with this petition.

6. A description and estimate of the value of any property of the adoptee is as follows:

____
.

7. ____ Consent by the adoptee is not required because the adoptee is not 12 years of age.
____ Consent by the adoptee is attached hereto.

8. The following persons are required to consent and the consent forms are attached:

____, mother of the minor child consents to this adoption.

____, father of the minor child consents to this adoption.

____, mother of the minor children was never married to the

father of ____.

The minor child's mother, ________________________ was not married to anyone at the time of the child's birth or conception.

9. The following person whose consent may be required has not consented. The facts/circumstances that excuse the lack of consent and would justify termination of parental rights are as follows:

____
____
____

WHEREFORE, I request that this Court terminate the parental rights of ____________________, ____ and ____; and enter a Final Judgment of Adoption of the Minor Child by Petitioners.

I understand that I am swearing or affirming under oath to the truthfulness of the claims made in this petition and that the punishment for knowingly making a false statement includes fines

and/or imprisonment.

Dated: ______________________

____
Signature of Petitioner,

Address: ___________________________
City, State, Zip: ______________________
Telephone Number: ___________________
Fax Number: ____________________________

STATE OF FLORIDA
COUNTY OF______________________

Sworn to or affirmed and signed before me on __________________by .
NOTARY PUBLIC or DEPUTY CLERK ____
[Print, type, or stamp commissioned name of notary or deputy clerk.] _____ Personally known _____
Produced identification
Type of identification produced ____________________________

IN THE CIRCUIT COURT OF THE ________________________ JUDICIAL CIRCUIT,
IN AND FOR __________________________ COUNTY, FLORIDA

Case No.: __________________________
Division: __________________________

IN THE MATTER OF THE ADOPTION OF

_______________________________________,
{use name to be given to child(ren)} Adoptee(s).

FINAL JUDGMENT OF ADOPTION BY RELATIVE(S)

Upon consideration of the Petition for Adoption by Relative(s) and the evidence presented, the Court finds that:

1. The Court has subject matter jurisdiction over the Joint Petition for Adoption by Relative(s).

2. The Court has jurisdiction over the minor child(ren) subject to the Joint Petition for Adoption by Relative(s).

3. Petitioner(s) desire the permanent responsibility of parent(s) in this adoption.

4. There is no pending litigation regarding the child(ren) in Florida or in any other state, nor is there any other person not a party to these proceedings who has or claims to have physical custody or rights to the minor child(ren).

5. The consent of the birth ( ) mother ( ) father who is not married to Petitioner is:
[**only** one]
____ attached to the petition
____ not required because he or she is deceased. A certified copy of the death certificate is attached.
____ waived because:
[all that apply]
____ the parent has deserted the child without means of identification or has abandoned the child.
____ the parent's rights have been terminated by a court of competent jurisdiction.
____ the parent has been declared incompetent and restoration of competency is medically improbable.
____ the legal guardian or lawful custodian of the adoptee(s), other than the birth parent, who has failed to respond in writing to a request for consent for a period of 60 days or the Court has examined the written reasons for withholding consent and has found the withholding of consent to be unreasonable.
____ other: ____.

6. The best interests of the child(ren) will be promoted by this adoption.

7. The minor child(ren) is (are) suitable for adoption by Petitioner(s).

NOW, THEREFORE, IT IS ORDERED that:

1. The minor child(ren) subject to the Petition is (are) declared to be the legal child(ren) of Petitioner(s),____ *{name}*

2. The minor child(ren) shall be the child(ren) and legal heir(s) at law of Petitioner(s), ____, *{name}* and shall be entitled to all rights and privileges, and subject to all obligations, of child(ren) born of Petitioner(s).

3. All legal relations between the adoptee(s) and the parent whose rights are being terminated and between the adoptee(s) and the relatives of that parent are terminated by this adoption, as are all parental rights and responsibilities of that birth parent.

4. This Final Judgment of Adoption creates a relationship between the adoptee(s) and Petitioner(s) and all relatives of Petitioner(s) that would have existed if the adoptee(s) was (were) a blood descendant of the Petitioner(s), born within wedlock, entitled to all rights and privileges thereof, and subject to all obligations of a child being born to Petitioner.(s)

5. The minor child(ren) shall hereafter be known as *{full legal name(s)}*:

____

ORDERED on _______________________.

____
CIRCUIT JUDGE

COPIES TO:
Petitioners (or their attorney)

APPENDIX III - SUPPLEMENTAL FORMS

You may need all or some of these supplemental forms depending on what happens after you file. For example, after filing you may discover that even though the biological parent promised he or she would sign the consent form, they never do. In that case, you would need to have that parent served by a sheriff or private process server.

Or, if you don't have a current address for the biological parent, you will need to conduct a diligent search for him or her. And if that parent is not located then he or she can be served by constructive service, through publication.

If the biological parent does not respond to the petition for adoption after being properly served either by personal service or constructive service, the next step is to file a Motion and Order for Default. This says to the court that the parent was properly served and failed to answer or respond in any way. The adoptive parent can then continue with the case and request a court hearing.

INSTRUCTIONS FOR FLORIDA FAMILY LAW RULES OF PROCEDURE FORM 12.910(a), SUMMONS: PERSONAL SERVICE ON AN INDIVIDUAL (09/12)

When should this form be used?

This form should be used to obtain **personal service** on the other **party** when you begin your lawsuit. **Service** is required for **all** documents filed in your case. Service means giving a copy of the required papers to the other party using the procedure that the law requires. Generally, there are two ways to make service: (1) personal service, or (2) service by e-mail, mail, or hand delivery. A third method for service is called **constructive service**; however, the relief a court may grant may be limited in a case where constructive service has been used.

The law requires that certain documents be served by **personal service** if personal service is possible. **Personal service** means that a summons (this form) and a copy of the forms you are filing with the court that must be personally served are delivered by a deputy sheriff or private process server

g. directly to the other party, **or**
h. to someone over the age of fifteen with whom the other party lives.

Personal service is required for **all petitions**, including petitions for modification. You cannot serve these papers on the other party yourself or by mail or hand delivery. Personal service must be made by the sheriff's department in the county where the other party lives or works or by a private process server certified in the county where the other party lives or works.

In many counties, there are private process servers who, for a fee, will personally serve the summons and other documents that require personal service. You should look under **process servers** in the yellow pages of the telephone book for a list of private process servers in your area. You may use a private process server to serve any paper required to be personally served in a family law case **except** a petition for injunction for protection against domestic or repeat violence.

How do I start?

When you begin your lawsuit, you need to complete this form (summons) and a **Process Service Memorandum**, Florida Supreme Court Approved Family Law Form 12.910(b). The forms should be typed or printed legibly in black ink. Next, you will need to take these forms and, if you have not already done so, **file** your petition with the **clerk of the circuit court** in the county where you live. You should keep a copy of the forms for your records. The clerk will sign the summons, and then the summons, a copy of the papers to be served, and the process service memorandum must be delivered to the appropriate sheriff's office or to a private process server for service on the other party.

IF THE OTHER PARTY LIVES IN THE COUNTY WHERE SUIT IS FILED: Ask the clerk in your county about any local procedures regarding service. Generally, if the other party lives in the county in which you are filing suit and you want the sheriff's department to serve the papers, you will file the summons along with a **Process Service Memorandum**, Florida Supreme Court Approved

Family Law Form 12.910(b), with the clerk and the clerk will forward those papers to the sheriff for service. Make sure that you attach a copy of the papers you want personally served to the summons. You may also need to provide the sheriff with a stamped envelope addressed to you. This will allow the sheriff to send the proof of service to you, after the sheriff serves your papers on the other party. However, in some counties the sheriff may send the proof of service directly to the clerk. If you are instructed to supply a self-addressed, stamped envelope and you receive the proof of service, you should file the proof of service with the clerk after you receive it from the sheriff. Also, you will need to find out how much the sheriff charges to serve the papers. Personal checks are not accepted. You should attach to the summons a cashier's check or money order made payable to the sheriff, and either give it to the clerk for delivery to the sheriff or send all of the paperwork and the fee to the sheriff yourself. The clerk will tell you which procedure to use. The costs for service may be waived if you are indigent.

If you want a private process server to serve the other party, you should still bring the summons to the clerk's office and have the clerk sign it for you. You should deliver the summons, along with the copy of your initial petition and any other papers to be served, and a **Process Service Memorandum**, Florida Supreme Court Approved Family Law Form 12.910(b), to the private process server. The private process server will charge you a fee for serving the papers. After service is complete, proof of service by the private process server must be filed with the clerk. You should discuss how this will occur with the private process server.

IF THE OTHER PARTY LIVES IN ANOTHER COUNTY: If the other party lives in another county, service needs to be made by a sheriff in the county where the other party lives or by a private process server certified in the county where the other party lives. Make sure that you attach a copy of the papers you want personally served to the summons as well as the **Process Service Memorandum**, Florida Supreme Court Approved Family Law Form 12.910(b). If you want the sheriff to serve the papers, the clerk may send your papers to that sheriff's office for you, or you may have to send the papers yourself. The clerk will tell you which procedure to use. Either way, you will need to provide the sheriff with a stamped envelope addressed to you. This will allow the sheriff to send the proof of service to you, after the sheriff serves your papers on the other party. You should file the proof of service with the clerk after you receive it from the sheriff. Also, you will need to find out how much the sheriff charges to serve the papers. Personal checks are not accepted. You should attach to the summons a cashier's check or money order made payable to the sheriff, and either give it to the clerk for delivery to the sheriff or send all of the paperwork and the fee to the sheriff yourself. The clerk will tell you which procedure to use. The costs for service may be waived if you are indigent.

If you want a private process server to serve the other party, you should still bring the summons to the clerk's office where the clerk will sign it for you. You should deliver the summons, along with the copy of your initial petition and any other papers to be served, and a **Process Service Memorandum**, Florida Supreme Court Approved Family Law Form 12.910(b), to the private process server. The private process server will charge you a fee for serving the papers. After service is complete, proof of service by the private process server must be filed with the clerk. You should discuss how this will occur with the private process server.

IF THE OTHER PARTY CANNOT BE LOCATED OR DOES NOT LIVE IN FLORIDA: If, after you have made a diligent effort to locate the other party, you absolutely cannot locate the other party, you may serve the other party by publication. Service by publication is also known as **constructive service**. You may also be able to use constructive service if the other party does not live in Florida. **However, Florida courts have only limited jurisdiction over a party who is served by constructive service and may have only limited jurisdiction over a party living outside of Florida regardless of whether that party is served by constructive or personal service**; that is, the judge's power to order the other party to do certain things may be limited. For example, the judge may be able to grant your request for a divorce, but the judge may not be able to address issues such as child support, spousal support (alimony), or division of property or debts.

Regardless of the type of service used, if the other party once lived in Florida but is living outside of Florida now, you should include in your petition a statement regarding the length of time the party lived in Florida, if any, and when. For example: Respondent last lived in Florida from *{date}* to
{date} ______________________.

This area of the law is very complex and you may need to consult with an attorney regarding the proper type of service to be used in your case if the other party does not live in Florida or cannot be located.

What happens when the papers are served on the other party?

The date and hour of service are written on the original summons and on all copies of it by the person making the service. The person who delivers the summons and copies of the petition must file a proof of service with the clerk or provide a proof of service to you for filing with the court. **It is your responsibility to make sure the proof of service has been returned to the clerk and placed in your case file.**

Where can I look for more information?

Before proceeding, you should read General Information for Self-Represented Litigants found at the beginning of these forms. For further information regarding service of process, see chapters 48 and 49, Florida Statutes, and rule 1.070, Florida Rules of Civil Procedure, as well as the instructions for **Notice of Action for Dissolution of Marriage (No Child or Financial Support)**, Florida Supreme Court Approved Family Law Form 12.913(a)(1), **Notice of Action for Family Cases with Minor Child(ren),** Florida Supreme Court Approved Family Law Form 12.913(a)(2), **Affidavit of Diligent Service and Inquiry**, Florida Family Law Rules of Procedure Form 12.913(b), and **Affidavit of Diligent Search,** Florida Family Law Rules of Procedure Form 12.913(c).

Special notes...

If you have been unable to obtain proper service on the other party within **120 days** after filing your lawsuit, the court will dismiss your lawsuit against the other party unless you can show the court a good reason why service was not made within **120 days**. For this reason, if you had the local sheriff serve the papers, you should check with the clerk every couple of weeks after completing the service papers to see if service has been completed. You may need to supply the sheriff with a new or better address. If you had a private process server or a sheriff in another county serve the papers, you should be in contact with that person or sheriff until you receive proof of service from that person or sheriff. You should then file the proof of service with the clerk immediately.

If the other party fails to respond, i.e., fails to file a written response with the court, within **20 days** after the service of the summons, you are entitled to request a **default**. See the instructions to **Motion for Default**, Florida Supreme Court Approved Family Law Form 12.922 (a), and **Default**, Florida Supreme Court Approved Family Law Form 12.922(b), for further information. You will need to file an **Affidavit of Military Service**, Florida Supreme Court Approved Family Law Form 12.912(b), before a default may be granted.

Remember, a person who is NOT an attorney is called a nonlawyer. If a nonlawyer helps you fill out these forms, that person must give you a copy of **Disclosure from Nonlawyer**, Florida Family Law Rules of Procedure Form 12.900(a), before he or she helps you. A nonlawyer helping you fill out these forms also **must** put his or her name, address, and telephone number on the bottom of the last page of every form he or she helps you complete.

IN THE CIRCUIT COURT OF THE _________________________ JUDICIAL CIRCUIT,
IN AND FOR _________________________ COUNTY, FLORIDA

Case No.: ____________________
Division: ____________________

__________________________________,
Petitioner,

and

__________________________________,
Respondent.

SUMMONS: PERSONAL SERVICE ON AN INDIVIDUAL ORDEN DE COMPARECENCIA: SERVICIO PERSONAL EN UN INDIVIDUO CITATION: L'ASSIGNATION PERSONAL SUR UN INDIVIDUEL

TO/PARA/A: *{enter other party's full legal name}* ______________________________,
{address (including city and state)/location for service} __________________________.

IMPORTANT

A lawsuit has been filed against you. You have **20 calendar days** after this summons is served on you to file a written response to the attached complaint/petition with the clerk of this circuit court, located at: *{street address}* ______________________________.
A phone call will not protect you. Your written response, including the case number given above and the names of the parties, must be **filed** if you want the Court to hear your side of the case.

If you do not file your written response on time, you may lose the case, and your wages, money, and property may be taken thereafter without further warning from the Court. There are other legal requirements. You may want to call an attorney right away. If you do not know an attorney, you may call an attorney referral service or a legal aid office (listed in the phone book).

If you choose to file a written response yourself, at the same time you file your written response to the Court, you must also serve a copy of your written response on the party serving this summons at:

{Name and address of party serving summons} ______________________________

____.

If the party serving summons has designated e-mail address(es) for service or is represented by an attorney, you may designate e-mail address(es) for service by or on you. Service must be in accordance with Florida Rule of Judicial Administration 2.516.

Copies of all court documents in this case, including orders, are available at the

Clerk of the Circuit Court's office. You may review these documents, upon request.

You must keep the Clerk of the Circuit Court's office notified of your current address. (You may file Designation of Current Mailing and E-mail Address, Florida Supreme Court Approved Family Law Form 12.915.) Future papers in this lawsuit will be served at the address on record at the clerk's office.

WARNING: Rule 12.285, Florida Family Law Rules of Procedure, requires certain automatic disclosure of documents and information. Failure to comply can result in sanctions, including dismissal or striking of pleadings.

IMPORTANTE

Usted ha sido demandado legalmente. Tiene veinte (20) dias, contados a partir del recibo de esta notificacion, para contestar la demanda adjunta, por escrito, y presentarla ante este tribunal. Localizado en: ____. Una llamada telefonica no lo protegera. Si usted desea que el tribunal considere su defensa, debe presentar su respuesta por escrito, incluyendo el numero del caso y los nombres de las partes interesadas. Si usted no contesta la demanda a tiempo, pudiese perder el caso y podria ser despojado de sus ingresos y propiedades, o privado de sus derechos, sin previo aviso del tribunal. Existen otros requisitos legales. Si lo desea, usted puede consultar a un abogado inmediatamente. Si no conoce a un abogado, puede llamar a una de las oficinas de asistencia legal que aparecen en la guia telefonica.

Si desea responder a la demanda por su cuenta, al mismo tiempo en que presente su respuesta ante el tribunal, usted debe enviar por correo o entregar una copia de su respuesta a la persona denominada abajo.

Si usted elige presentar personalmente una respuesta por escrito, en el mismo momento que usted presente su respuesta por escrito al Tribunal, usted debe enviar por correo o llevar una copia de su respuesta por escrito a la parte entregando esta orden de comparencencia a:

Nombre y direccion de la parte que entrega la orden de comparencencia: _____________

____.

Copias de todos los documentos judiciales de este caso, incluyendo las ordenes, estan disponibles en la oficina del Secretario de Juzgado del Circuito [Clerk of the Circuit Court's office]. Estos documentos pueden ser revisados a su solicitud.

Usted debe de manener informada a la oficina del Secretario de Juzgado del Circuito de su direccion actual. (Usted puede presentar ______ el Formulario: Ley de Familia de la Florida 12.915, Florida Supreme Court Approved Family Law Form 12.915, Designation of Current Mailing and E-mail Address.) Los papelos que se presenten en el futuro en esta demanda judicial seran env ados por correo a la direccion que este registrada en la oficina del Secretario.

ADVERTENCIA: Regla 12.285 (Rule 12.285), de las Reglas de Procedimiento de Ley de Familia de la Florida [Florida Family Law Rules of Procedure], requiere cierta revelacion automatica de documentos e informacion. El incumplimient, puede resultar en sanciones, incluyendo la desestimacion o anulacion de los alegatos.

IMPORTANT

Des poursuites judiciaries ont ete entreprises contre vous. Vous avez 20 jours consecutifs a partir de la date de l'assignation de cette citation pour deposer une reponse ecrite a la plainte ci-jointe aupres de ce tribunal. Qui se trouve a: *{L'Adresse}* __________ . Un simple coup de telephone est insuffisant pour vous proteger; vous etes obliges de deposer votre reponse ecrite, avec mention du numero de dossier ci-dessus et du nom des parties nommees ici, si vous souhaitez que le tribunal entende votre cause. Si vous ne deposez pas votre reponse ecrite dans le delai requis, vous risquez de perdre la cause ainsi que votre salaire, votre argent, et vos biens peuvent etre saisis par la suite, sans aucun preavis ulterieur du tribunal. Il y a d'autres obligations juridiques et vous pouvez requerir les services immediats d'un avocat. Si vous ne connaissez pas d'avocat, vous pourriez telephoner a un service de reference d'avocats ou a un bureau d'assistance juridique (figurant a l'annuaire de telephones).

Si vous choisissez de deposer vous-meme une reponse ecrite, il vous faudra egalement, en meme temps que cette formalite, faire parvenir ou expedier une copie au carbone ou une photocopie de votre reponse ecrite a la partie qui vous depose cette citation.

Nom et adresse de la partie qui depose cette citation: ______________________________

____

Les photocopies de tous les documents tribunals de cette cause, y compris des arrets, sont disponible au bureau du greffier. Vous pouvez revue ces documents, sur demande.

Il faut aviser le greffier de votre adresse actuelle. (Vous pouvez deposer Florida Supreme Court Approved Family Law Form 12.915, Designation of Current Mailing and E-mail Address.) Les documents de l'avenir de ce proces seront envoyer a l'adresse que vous donnez au bureau du greffier.

ATTENTION: La regle 12.285 des regles de procedure du droit de la famille de la Floride exige que l'on remette certains renseignements et certains documents a la partie adverse. Tout refus de les fournir pourra donner lieu a des sanctions, y compris le rejet ou la suppression d'un ou de plusieurs actes de procedure.

THE STATE OF FLORIDA
TO EACH SHERIFF OF THE STATE: You are commanded to serve this summons and a copy of the complaint in this lawsuit on the above-named person.

DATED: ______________________

CLERK OF THE CIRCUIT COURT

(SEAL)

By: ________________________________
Deputy Clerk

INSTRUCTIONS FOR FLORIDA SUPREME COURT APPROVED FAMILY LAW FORM 12.910(b), PROCESS SERVICE MEMORANDUM (11/15)

When should this form be used?

You should use this form to give the sheriff's department (or private process server) instructions for serving the other **party** in your case with the **Summons: Personal Service on an Individual**, Florida Family Law Rules of Procedure Form 12.910(a), and other papers to be served. On this form you can tell the sheriff's department the best times to find the person at work and/or at home. You can also include a map to the other person's home or work place to help the sheriff find the person and deliver the summons. Do not forget to attach to the summons a copy of your initial petition and any other papers you want personally served on the other party.

This form should be typed or printed in black ink. After completing this form, you should **file** the original with the **clerk of the circuit court** in the county where your petition was filed and attach a copy to the **Summons: Personal Service on an Individual**, Florida Family Law Rules of Procedure Form 12.910(a). You should also keep a copy for your records.

IMPORTANT INFORMATION REGARDING E-FILING

The Florida Rules of Judicial Administration now require that all petitions, pleadings, and documents be filed electronically except in certain circumstances. **Self-represented litigants may file petitions or other pleadings or documents electronically; however, they are not required to do so.** If you choose to file your pleadings or other documents electronically, you must do so in accordance with Florida Rule of Judicial Administration 2.525, and you must follow the procedures of the judicial circuit in which you file. **The rules and procedures should be carefully read and followed.**

Where can I look for more information?

Before proceeding, you should read General Information for Self-Represented Litigants found at the beginning of these forms. You should read the instructions for **Summons: Personal Service on an Individual**, Florida Family Law Rules of Procedure Form 12.910(a), for additional information.

IMPORTANT INFORMATION REGARDING E-SERVICE ELECTION

After the initial service of process of the petition or supplemental petition by the Sheriff or certified process server, the Florida Rules of Judicial Administration now require that all documents required or permitted to be served on the other party must be served by electronic mail (e-mail) except in certain circumstances. **You must strictly comply with the format requirements set forth in the Rules of Judicial Administration.** If you elect to participate in electronic service, which means serving or receiving pleadings by electronic mail (e-mail), or through the Florida Courts E-Filing Portal, you **must** review Florida Rule of Judicial Administration 2.516. You may find this rule at www.flcourts.org through the link to the Rules of Judicial Administration provided under either Family Law Forms: Getting Started, or Rules of Court in the A-Z Topical Index.

SELF-REPRESENTED LITIGANTS MAY SERVE DOCUMENTS BY E-MAIL; HOWEVER, THEY ARE NOT REQUIRED TO DO SO. If a self-represented litigant elects to serve and receive documents by e-mail, the procedures must always be followed once the initial election is made.

To serve and receive documents by e-mail, you must designate your e-mail addresses by using the **Designation of Current Mailing and E-mail Address**, Florida Supreme Court Approved Family Law Form 12.915, and you must provide your e-mail address on each form on which your signature appears. Please **CAREFULLY** read the rules and instructions for: **Certificate of Service (General),** Florida Supreme Court Approved Family Law Form 12.914; **Designation of Current Mailing and E-mail Address**, Florida Supreme Court Approved Family Law Form 12.915; and Florida Rule of Judicial Administration 2.516.

Special notes...

If you fear that disclosing your address would put you in danger because you are the victim of sexual battery, aggravated child abuse, stalking, aggravated stalking, harassment, aggravated battery, or domestic violence, you should complete a **Request for Confidential Filing of Address**, Florida Supreme Court Approved Family Law Form 12.980(h), file it with the clerk, and write confidential in the space provided on the petition.

Nonlawyer. Remember, a person who is NOT an attorney is called a nonlawyer. If a nonlawyer helps you fill out these forms, that person must give you a copy of **Disclosure from Nonlawyer**, Florida Family Law Rules of Procedure Form 12.900 (a), before he or she helps you. A nonlawyer helping you fill out these forms also **must** put his or her name, address, and telephone number on the bottom of the last page of every form he or she helps you complete.

IN THE CIRCUIT COURT OF THE ____________________ JUDICIAL CIRCUIT,
IN AND FOR ______________________ COUNTY, FLORIDA

Case No.: ________________________

Division: ________________________

______________________________,
Petitioner,

and

______________________________,
Respondent,

PROCESS SERVICE MEMORANDUM

TO: _____ Sheriff of ______________________ County, Florida;
____________________ Division
____________________ Private process server:
____

Please serve the *{name of document(s)}*
____
____
in the above-styled cause upon:
Party: *{full legal name}*
____
Address or location for service:
____
____
Work Address:
____
____

If the party to be served owns, has, and/or is known to have guns or other weapons, describe what type of weapon(s):
____

SPECIAL INSTRUCTIONS:
____
____
____
____
____

Dated: ____________________

____
Signature of Party

*Printed Name: _______________
*Address: ____________________
*City, State, Zip: _______________
*Telephone Number: ___________
*Fax Number: ________________
*Designated E-mail Address(es)_
____
____

*** Please see the Special Notes section in the instructions to this form regarding Florida Supreme Court Approved Family Law Form 12.980(h), Request for Confidential Filing of Address, which may be used if you need to keep your addresses or telephone numbers confidential for safety reasons.**

IF A NONLAWYER HELPED YOU FILL OUT THIS FORM, HE/SHE MUST FILL IN THE BLANKS BELOW:
[fill in **all** blanks] This form was prepared for the Petitioner. This form was completed with the assistance of:
{name of individual} ____,
{name of business} ____,
*{address}*____,
*{city}*______________, *{state}* ____, *{zip code}*__________, *{telephone number}*
____

INSTRUCTIONS FOR FLORIDA SUPREME COURT APPROVED FAMILY LAW FORMS 12.922(a), MOTION FOR DEFAULT, AND 12.922(b), DEFAULT (11/15)

When should these forms be used?

If the other **party** has failed to **file** or **serve** any documents within 20 days after the date of service of your **petition**, you may ask the **clerk of the circuit court** to enter a **default** against him or her by filling out this form and filing it with the court. Generally, a default allows you to obtain an earlier **final hearing** to finish your case. Once the default is signed by the clerk, you can request a **trial** or final hearing in your case.

To obtain a default, you will need to complete **Motion for Default**, Florida Supreme Court Approved Family Law Form 12.922(a). You will then need to file your motion for default along with the **Default**, Florida Supreme Court Approved Family Law Form 12.922(b), so that the clerk can enter a default for you if your motion is proper.

This form should be typed or printed in black ink. After completing this form, you should file the original with the **clerk of the circuit court** in the county where you filed your petition and keep a copy for your records.

IMPORTANT INFORMATION REGARDING E-FILING

The Florida Rules of Judicial Administration now require that all petitions, pleadings, and documents be filed electronically except in certain circumstances. **Self-represented litigants may file petitions or other pleadings or documents electronically; however, they are not required to do so.** If you choose to file your pleadings or other documents electronically, you must do so in accordance with Florida Rule of Judicial Administration 2.525, and you must follow the procedures of the judicial circuit in which you file. **The rules and procedures should be carefully read and followed.**

What should I do next?

After the default has been entered, you must ask for a hearing, so that the **judge** can consider your petition. To do this, you must contact the clerk's office, **family law intake staff**, or **judicial assistant** to schedule a hearing and file a **Notice of Hearing (General)**, Florida Supreme Court Approved Family Law Form 12.923, with the clerk. A copy of the notice of hearing must be mailed, e-mailed, or hand-delivered to each party in the case. **You must send a notice of final hearing to the defaulted party.**

IMPORTANT INFORMATION REGARDING E-SERVICE ELECTION

After the initial service of process of the petition or supplemental petition by the Sheriff or certified process server, the Florida Rules of Judicial Administration now require that all documents required or permitted to be served on the other party must be served by electronic mail (e-mail) except in certain circumstances. **You must strictly comply with the format requirements set forth in the Rules of Judicial Administration.** If you elect to participate in electronic service, which means serving or receiving pleadings by electronic mail (e-mail), or through the Florida Courts E-Filing Portal, you **must** review Florida Rule of Judicial Administration 2.516. You may find this rule at www.flcourts.org through the link to the Rules of Judicial Administration provided under either Family Law Forms: Getting Started, or Rules of Court in the A-Z Topical Index.

SELF-REPRESENTED LITIGANTS MAY SERVE DOCUMENTS BY E-MAIL; HOWEVER, THEY ARE NOT REQUIRED TO DO SO. If a self-represented litigant elects to serve and receive documents by e-mail, the procedures must always be followed once the initial election is made.

To serve and receive documents by e-mail, you must designate your e-mail addresses by using the **Designation of Current Mailing and E-mail Address**, Florida Supreme Court Approved Family Law Form 12.915, and you must provide your e-mail address on each form on which your signature appears. Please **CAREFULLY** read the rules and instructions for: **Certificate of Service (General),** Florida Supreme Court Approved Family Law Form 12.914; **Designation of Current Mailing and E-mail Address**, Florida Supreme Court Approved Family Law Form 12.915; and Florida Rule of Judicial Administration 2.516.

Where can I look for more information?

Before proceeding, you should read General Information for Self-Represented Litigants found at the beginning of these forms. For further information, see Florida Rules of Civil Procedure 1.500, concerning defaults and Rule 1.140, concerning the time within which a party can file an answer or other responsive pleading to a petition. See also Florida Family Law Rule of Procedure 12.080.

Special notes...

Remember, a person who is NOT an attorney is called a nonlawyer. If a nonlawyer helps you fill out these forms, that person must give you a copy of **Disclosure from Nonlawyer**, Florida Family Law Rules of Procedure Form 12.900 (a), before he or she helps you. A nonlawyer helping you fill out these forms also **must** put his or her name, address, and telephone number on the bottom of the last page of every form he or she helps you complete.

IN THE CIRCUIT COURT OF THE ____________________ JUDICIAL CIRCUIT,
IN AND FOR ______________________ COUNTY, FLORIDA

Case No.: ______________________

Division: ______________________

______________________,
Petitioner,

and

______________________,
Respondent,

MOTION FOR DEFAULT

TO THE CLERK OF THE CIRCUIT COURT:

PLEASE ENTER A DEFAULT AGAINST RESPONDENT WHO HAS FAILED TO RESPOND TO THE PETITION.

I certify that a copy of this document was ( ) mailed ( ) faxed and mailed ( ) e-mailed ( ) hand-delivered to the person(s) listed below on *{date}* ____________________.

Other party or his/her attorney:
Name: ______________________
Address: ______________________
City, State, Zip: ______________________
Fax Number: ______________________
Designated E-mail Address(es): ______________________
____

____
Signature of Party
Printed Name: ______________________
Address: ______________________
City, State, Zip: ______________________
Telephone Number: ______________________
Fax Number: ______________________
Designated E-mail Address(es): ______________________
____

IF A NONLAWYER HELPED YOU FILL OUT THIS FORM, HE/SHE MUST FILL IN THE BLANKS BELOW:
[fill in **all** blanks] This form was prepared for the: *{choose only **one**}* (   ) Petitioner (   ) Respondent
This form was completed with the assistance of:
{name of individual } ____,
{name of business} ____,
{address} ____,
{city} _______________, *{state}* ____, *{zip code}*_________,*{telephone number}*
_______________.

IN THE CIRCUIT COURT OF THE ______________________ JUDICIAL CIRCUIT,
IN AND FOR _______________________ COUNTY, FLORIDA

Case No.: ________________________
Division: _________________________

_______________________________________,
Petitioner,

and

_______________________________________,
Respondent,

DEFAULT

A default is entered in this action against Respondent for failure to serve or file a response or any paper as is required by law.

Dated:____________

CLERK OF THE CIRCUIT COURT
(SEAL)

By:

____
Deputy Clerk

I certify that a copy of this document was ( ) mailed ( ) faxed and mailed ( ) e-mailed ( ) hand-delivered to the person(s) listed below on *{date}* ____________________.

Other party or his/her attorney:
Name: ____________________________________
Address: __________________________________
City, State, Zip: ____________________________
Fax Number: ________________________________
Designated E-mail Address(es):____________________

____
Signature of Party
Printed Name: ___________________________
Address: _______________________________
City, State, Zip: _________________________
Telephone Number:_______________________
Fax Number:____________________________
Designated E-mail
Address(es):____________________________
____

INSTRUCTIONS FOR FLORIDA FAMILY LAW RULES OF PROCEDURE FORM 12.913(c), AFFIDAVIT OF DILIGENT SEARCH (11/12)

When should this form be used?

This form is to be used with **Notice of Action For Family Cases With Minor Child(ren)**, Florida Supreme C ourt Approved Family Law Form 12.913(a)(2), to obtain **constructive service** (also called service by public ation) on the legal father in any action or proceeding to determine paternity which may result in termination of the legal father's parental rights.

The legal father is entitled to actual notice of the proceedings when possible. When it is necessary to use constructive notice, it must be given in a way that is likely to provide actual notice. You must disclose the last known address of the legal father. A last known address cannot be unknown. This form includes a checklist of places you must look for information on the location of the legal father. You have to look in all of these places, and the court must believe that you have made a very serious effort to get information about the person's location and that you have followed up on any information you received.

This form should be typed or printed in black ink. After completing this form, you should sign the form before a **notary public** or **deputy clerk**. You should **file** the original and a **Notice of Action For Family Cases With Minor Child(ren),** Florida Supreme Court Approved Family Law Form 12.913(a)(2), with the **clerk of the circuit court** in the county where your petition for dissolution of marriage is filed. You should keep a copy for your records.

Where can I look for more information?

Before proceeding, you should read General Information for Self-Represented Litigants found at the beginning of these forms. For further information, see rule 12.070, Florida Family Law Rules of Procedure, chapter 49, Florida Statutes, and section 409.257, Florida Statutes.

Special notes...

Remember, a person who is NOT an attorney is called a nonlawyer. If a nonlawyer helps you fill out these forms, that person must give you a copy of **Disclosure from Nonlawyer**, Florida Family Law Rules of Procedure Form 12.900(a), before he or she helps you. A nonlawyer helping you fill out these forms also **must** put his or her name, address, and telephone number on the bottom of the last page of every form he or she helps you complete.

IN THE CIRCUIT COURT OF THE ______________________ JUDICIAL CIRCUIT,
IN AND FOR ______________________________COUNTY, FLORIDA

Case No.: ______________________
Division:________________________

_________________________________,
Petitioner,

and

_________________________________,
Respondent.

AFFIDAVIT OF DILIGENT SEARCH

I, *{full legal name}*________________________________, being sworn, certify that the following information is true:

i. The last known address of the child(ren)'s legal father *{name}*______________________,
as of *{date}*_____________________________, was:
Address __________________________ City____________ State__________ Zip ______
Telephone No. ____________________ Fax No. _______________________.

His last known employment, as of *{date}* _________________, was:
Name of Employer

____

Address ___________________________ City ___________ State ________ Zip
____
Telephone No. ____________________ Fax No. ______________________

j. The legal father is over the age of 18.

k. The legal father's current residence is not known and cannot be determined, although I have made a diligent search and inquiry to locate him through the following:
You must search ALL of the following sources of information and state the results.

____ United States Post Office inquiry through the Freedom of Information Act for the legal father's current address or any previous address.
Result of search:____

____ Last known employment of the legal father, including name and address of employer.
Result of search:____

____ Regulatory agencies, including professional or occupational licensing, in the area where the legal father last resided.
Result of search:____________________

____ Names and addresses of relatives to the extent such can be reasonably obtained from the petitioner or other sources, contacts with those relatives and inquiry as to the legal father's last known address. You are to follow up any leads of any addresses where the legal father may have moved.
Result of search:

____

____ Information about the legal father's possible death and, if dead, the date and location.
Result of search:____

____ Telephone listings in the area where the legal father last resided.
Result of search:

____

____ Law enforcement agencies in the area where the legal father last resided.
Result of search:

____

____ Highway Patrol records in the state where the legal father last resided.
Result of search:

____

____ Department of Corrections records in the state where the legal father last resided.
Result of search: _______________________________________

____

____ Hospitals in the last known area of the legal father's residence.
Result of search:

____

____ Records of utility companies, which include water, sewer, cable TV, and electric in the last known area of the legal father's residence.
Result of search:

____

____ Records of the Armed Forces of the U.S. and their response as to whether or not there is any information about the legal father. (See Florida Supreme Court Approved Family Law Form 12.912(a), Memorandum for Certificate of Military Service.)
Result of search:

____

____ Records of the tax assessor's and tax collector's office in the area where the legal father last resided.
Result of search:____

____ Search of one Internet databank locator service.
Result of search:

____

____ Title IV-D (child support enforcement) agency records in the state of the legal

father's last known address.
Result of search:

____

I understand that I am swearing or affirming under oath to the truthfulness of the claims made in this affidavit and that the punishment for knowingly making a false statement includes fines and/or imprisonment.

Dated:___________________________

____

Signature of Petitioner
Printed Name: ________________________

Address: ____________________________

City, State, Zip: ________________________

Telephone Number: ____________________

Fax Number: __________________________
E-mail Address(es):______________________

STATE OF FLORIDA
COUNTY OF ____________________

Sworn to or affirmed and signed before me on __________ by
__________________________.

____

NOTARY PUBLIC or DEPUTY CLERK

[Print, type, or stamp commissioned name of notary or deputy clerk.]

____ Personally known
____ Produced identification
Type of identification produced __________________________

IF A NONLAWYER HELPED YOU FILL OUT THIS FORM, HE/SHE MUST FILL IN THE BLANKS BELOW: [fill in **all** blanks]
This form was prepared for: *{choose only* ***one****}* ( ) Petitioner ( ) Respondent
This form was completed with the assistance of:
{ name of individual} ____,
{name of business} ____,
{address} ____,
{city} ____________________,*{state}* __________, *{telephone number}*
__________________.

INSTRUCTIONS FOR FLORIDA SUPREME COURT APPROVED FAMILY LAW FORM 12.913(a)(2) NOTICE OF ACTION FOR FAMILY CASES WITH MINOR CHILD(REN) (11/15)

When should this form be used?

This form may be used to obtain **constructive service** (also called service by publication) in an action involving a parenting plan for a minor child under chapter 61, Florida Statutes; an action to determine temporary custody by extended family under chapter 751, Florida Statutes; and termination of a legal father's parental rights when another man is alleged to be the biological father. "Parenting plan" means a document created to govern the relationship between the parents relating to decisions that must be made regarding the minor child and must contain a time-sharing schedule for the parents and child. Section 61.046(14), Florida Statutes. You may use constructive service if you do not know where the other party lives or if the other party lives outside Florida and you are unable to obtain **personal service**. Constructive notice will allow the court to grant the relief requested, but personal service is required before a court can order payment or termination of **child support,** spousal support (**alimony**), or costs. If you are asking the court to decide how real or personal property located in Florida should be divided, the **Notice of Action** must include a specific description of the property. If you use constructive service, the court can grant only limited relief because its jurisdiction is limited. This is a complicated area of the law and you should consult an attorney before using constructive service.

You should complete this form by typing or printing the appropriate information in black ink. You must insert the other party's name and last known address and then **file** this form with the **clerk of the circuit court** in the county where your petition was filed. You must also complete and file an **Affidavit of Diligent Search and Inquiry**. Use Florida Family Law Rules of Procedure Form 12.913(b) unless you are serving the legal father in a paternity case where another man is alleged to be the biological father, in which case, you must use Form 12.913(c). You should keep a copy for your records.

IMPORTANT INFORMATION REGARDING E-FILING

The Florida Rules of Judicial Administration now require that all petitions, pleadings, and documents be filed electronically except in certain circumstances. **Self-represented litigants may file petitions or other pleadings or documents electronically; however, they are not required to do so.** If you choose to file your pleadings or other documents electronically, you must do so in accordance with Florida Rule of Judicial Administration 2.525, and you must follow the procedures of the judicial circuit in which you file. **The rules and procedures should be carefully read and followed.**

After the **Affidavit of Diligent Search and Inquiry**, Family Law Rules of Procedure Form 12.913(b) or 12.913(c), is filed, the clerk will sign this form. You will need to publish notice once each week for four consecutive weeks in a "qualified" newspaper in the county where the case is pending. When in doubt, ask the clerk which newspapers are "qualified." The newspaper will charge you for this service. If you cannot afford to pay the cost of publishing this notice, you may ask the clerk to post the notice at a place designated for such postings. You will need to file an **Application for Determination of Civil Indigent Status,** which you can obtain from the clerk. If the clerk determines that you cannot afford these costs, the clerk will post the notice of action. If your case involves termination of a legal father's parental rights when another man is alleged to be the biological father, you need to publish the notice only in the county where the legal father was last known to have resided. You are responsible for locating a "qualified" newspaper in the county where the other party last resided and paying the cost of publication.

Where can I look for more information?

Before proceeding, you should read "General Information for Self-Represented Litigants" found at the beginning of these forms. For further information, see rule 12.070, Florida Family Law Rules of Procedure, rule 1.070, Florida Rules of Civil Procedure, sections 61.501–61.542, Florida Statutes and chapter 49, Florida Statutes.

IMPORTANT INFORMATION REGARDING E-SERVICE ELECTION

After the initial service of process of the petition or supplemental petition by the Sheriff or certified process server, the Florida Rules of Judicial Administration now require that all documents required or permitted to be served on the other party must be served by electronic mail (e-mail) except in certain circumstances. **You must strictly comply with the format requirements set forth in the Rules of Judicial Administration.** If you elect to participate in electronic service, which means serving or receiving pleadings by electronic mail (e-mail), or through the Florida Courts E-Filing Portal, you **must** review Florida Rule of Judicial Administration 2.516. You may find this rule at www.flcourts.org through the link to the Rules of Judicial Administration provided under either Family Law Forms: Getting Started, or Rules of Court in the A-Z Topical Index.

SELF-REPRESENTED LITIGANTS MAY SERVE DOCUMENTS BY E-MAIL; HOWEVER, THEY ARE NOT REQUIRED TO DO SO. If a self-represented litigant elects to serve and receive documents by e- mail, the procedures must always be followed once the initial election is made.

To serve and receive documents by e-mail, you must designate your e-mail addresses by using the **Designation of Current Mailing and E-mail Address**, Florida Supreme Court Approved Family Law Form 12.915, and you must provide your e-mail address on each form on which your signature appears. Please **CAREFULLY** read the rules and instructions for: **Certificate of Service (General),** Florida Supreme Court Approved Family Law Form 12.914; **Designation of Current Mailing and E- mail Address**, Florida Supreme Court Approved Family Law Form 12.915; and Florida Rule of Judicial Administration 2.516.

Special notes...

If the other party fails to respond to your **petition** within the time limit stated in the notice of action that is published or posted, you are entitled to request a **default**. (See **Motion for Default**, Florida Supreme Court Approved Family Law Form 12.922(a), and **Default**, Florida Supreme Court Approved Family Law Form 12.922(b).) Remember, a person who is NOT an attorney is called a nonlawyer. If a nonlawyer helps you fill out these forms, that person must give you a copy of **Disclosure from Nonlawyer**, Florida Family Law Rules of Procedure Form 12.900(a), before he or she helps you. A nonlawyer helping you fill out these forms also **must** put his or her name, address, and telephone number on the bottom of the last page of every form he or she helps you complete.

IN THE CIRCUIT COURT OF THE ____________________ JUDICIAL CIRCUIT,
IN AND FOR _____________________ COUNTY, FLORIDA

Case No.:
____
Division: .
____

______________________________,
Petitioner,

and

______________________________,
Respondent,

NOTICE OF ACTION FOR

{Specify action}
____

TO: *{name of Respondent}*
____
{Respondent's last known address}
____

YOU ARE NOTIFIED that an action for *{identify the type of case}* ____________________________ has been filed against you and that you are required to serve a copy of your written defenses, if any, to it on *{name of Petitioner}* ____, whose address is ____, on or before *{date}* _______________, and file the original with the clerk of this Court at *{clerk's address}* ____ ______, before service on Petitioner or immediately thereafter. **If you fail to do so, a default may be entered against you for the relief demanded in the petition.**

{If applicable, insert the legal description of real property, a specific description of personal property, and the name of the county in Florida where the property is located}
____
____
____

Copies of all court documents in this case, including orders, are available at the Clerk of the Circuit Court's office. You may review these documents upon request.

You must keep the Clerk of the Circuit Court's office notified of your current

address. (You may file Designation of Current Mailing and E-Mail Address, Florida Supreme Court Approved Family Law Form 12.915.) Future papers in this lawsuit will be mailed or e-mailed to the addresses on record at the clerk's office.WARNING: Rule 12.285, Florida Family Law Rules of Procedure, requires certain automatic disclosure of documents and information. Failure to comply can result in sanctions, including dismissal or striking of pleadings.

Dated: ______________________ CLERK OF THE CIRCUIT COURT

By:

____

Deputy Clerk

IF A NONLAWYER HELPED YOU FILL OUT THIS FORM, HE/SHE MUST FILL IN THE BLANKS BELOW:

[fill in **all** blanks] This form was prepared for the Petitioner.
This form was completed with the assistance of:
{name of individual}, ____,
{name of business}____,
{address} ____,
{city}________________,{state} _____, {zip code}_________,{telephone number}________________.

Author's Note

Dear Readers,

I hope you've found this book helpful and informative. I have prepared adoption forms for hundreds of Florida family adoptions over the past six years. Family adoptions are one of my favorite types of document sets to prepare, because they always have a joyous ending. I would love to hear your feedback, questions, and comments. Please contact me directly. staff@faldp.org or 800-515-0496.

Best Regards,

Ruth Tick, Director FALDP, LLC
FALDP Certification #161

www.ingramcontent.com/pod-product-compliance
Ingram Content Group UK Ltd.
Pitfield, Milton Keynes, MK11 3LW, UK
UKHW051137260726
13967UKWH00010B/3103

9 781304 582430